Charley Dickey's Dove Hunting

GALAHAD BOOKS · NEW YORK CITY

Published by arrangement with Oxmoor House, Inc.
ISBN: 0-88365-336-2

Copyright © 1975 by Oxmoor House, Inc.
Book Division of the Progressive Farmer Company
P.O. Box 2463, Birmingham, Alabama 35202

All rights reserved. No part of this book may be reproduced in any form by any means without prior written permission of the Publisher, excepting brief quotes used in connection with reviews written specifically for inclusion in a magazine or newspaper.

Library of Congress Catalog Number: 75-12121

Manufactured in the United States of America

First Printing 1976

Dove Hunting

Editor: Lee Greenwood
Cover Photograph: Charley Dickey
Illustrations: Ralph Mark

To Dave and all those boys
in the back room.

Acknowledgments

Special thanks are extended to the following people for their assistance on various parts of this book: Papa Jack Lauder, James Fuller, Bubber Harden, Jack Wingate, Jimmie McDaniel, Fred Stanberry, Cader Cox, George Moore, Barbara Dickey, Earle Frye, James L. Ruos, Roy E. Tomlinson, Fred Moses, George Fuller, and David Dale Dickey. I am also very grateful for the technical information furnished by state game and fish departments in the 32 states which have dove and bandtail pigeon hunting and by the Fish and Wildlife Service, United States Department of the Interior. I would like to commend these agencies for the excellent way in which they manage our fish and wildlife resources.

Introduction	5
Life History of the Mourning Dove	7
Types of Dove Hunting	21
A Place to Hunt	32
Guns and Shells	38
Other Equipment	50
Dogs	56
Selecting a Shooting Site	65
Managing a Hunt	75
How to Hit a Dove	80
More on Shooting	88
How Hunting Regulations are Set	98
Field Care, Dressing, and Recipes	102
Appendix	111

Introduction

From my own hunting experiences and those of many experts I've shot with, I'm going to tell you how to hunt doves, if you are a beginner, and how to improve your score, if you are already a dove hunter.

The mourning dove is the most popular game bird of all upland and migratory birds in America. About 50 million are bagged every season with no damaging effect on the basic breeding flock which replenishes the supply each spring and summer.

Although hunters generally can't agree on anything related to their favorite sport, they do concur that the dove is the hardest of all game birds to hit. At a speed of 35 to 45 miles an hour (50 to 60 with a tailwind), it zigs, zags, darts, dives, climbs and is most uncooperative at the exact instant when you start to pull the trigger.

Such flight patterns are naturally a delight to the manufacturers of shotgun shells. Depending upon which survey you believe, it takes the average hunter five to eight shells to pick up one dove.

Speed and maneuverability have not only helped the dove survive the gunning fields but have also earned it the formidable reputation of being the hardest game bird on the North American continent to bring down consistently. This reputation often spooks a hunter into defeating himself even before he reaches his blind in a field swarming with hungry doves.

Another defense for the dove, if the shooting pressure becomes too intense in one area, is simply to move to another area, to migrate as much as 100 miles. The best defense for the survival of the species (not the individual bird), however, is the adult bird's ability to bring off one to six hatches of young a year.

The "gray ghost," so called by hunters who use polite language, is all the challenge most shotgunners want. The English language is lacking in oral expressions needed by hunters who miss both easy and difficult shots, and I once heard a missionary revert to Swahili to relieve his exasperation.

Although not versed in that language, I knew from his tone what he was saying. I tapped him gently on the shoulder and said, "Father, you have sinned." His red, sweating face glowered at me and then relaxed into a smile. "Yes, my son, I have been sorely tempted. Could you possibly let me have a couple more boxes of shells?"

I reached into my surplus GI ammo box and handed him a new supply. "Bless you, my son," he said. "Stay low! Here comes another flock of those darting sons of, uh, nature!"

Having tasted the bitter dust of frustration from Pennsylvania corn fields to safflower stubble in California to milo patches in Florida, I have much sympathy for hunters who have difficulty in hitting these wisps of darting feathers.

On one glorious afternoon in South Carolina, I bagged 12 doves with 13 shots, a feat I have since related to every hunter I could corner. A week later in Oklahoma, while shooting in a high wind across a peanut field, I shot more than 90 shells with results so meager that I dodged the other hunters as I left the field so that no one could ask me how many I had bagged.

Certainly I had enough experience to have shot respectably that blustery afternoon—usually anyone who has hunted doves for several years will generally have learned how to handle most of the prospects that come within shooting range. I knew what I was supposed to do on each shot, but I had defeated myself because much of wing shooting is a mental game. Hank Aaron can knock a ball into the centerfield bleachers one time and strike out the next two times at bat. A dove shooter can smoothly bag a double and then miss seven or eight easy shots in a row. But that's what makes dove shooting forever interesting and challenging.

This book will discuss your quarry, your equipment, and the best methods of bringing down the former with the latter. Following its procedures and advice will assure you of many successful days afield.

Most types of dove hunting are a social way of enjoying the outdoors with one partner or a group of 10 to 40. When you shoot, someone is always watching. If you shoot well, you may receive a compliment; if you perform poorly, your companions will gleefully shout remarks they consider hilarious. All hunters on stage like to shoot well.

However, there is much more to going afield than merely bagging a limit. Are you fair to all your hunting partners and the landowner? Do you obey the federal and state regulations? Most of all, are you fair to your quarry—taking only those shots in range that you can kill cleanly? In other words, do you display good sportsmanship? If you are a good sportsman, you enjoy living with yourself, and that's what really counts.

Life History of the Mourning Dove

The mourning dove does not get its name from the wake of hunters it leaves mourning their missed shots. Even when a dove is happy, its call is lonesome and plaintive, much like an owl "who-whoing" in the distance. It even sounds mournful when making love, which is reason enough to give it a sad name.

Although some people call it a turtledove, the mourning dove doesn't mind being confused with its European relative. There are two races of mourning doves in the United States, the Eastern and the Western. The Western race is lighter colored than its Eastern brother. The two overlap in range but have never had any integration problems. Wildlife biologists worry a lot about classifying birds, but hunters are more concerned with bagging a limit or shooting respectably (when others are watching).

The mourning dove is part of the pigeon family *Columbidae* with kinfolk all over the world. Of the 500 or so species, there are about 20 in the United States. The mourning dove was taken to Hawaii from the mainland to join such native cousins as the lace-necked and barred doves. Mourning doves are also related to the common domestic pigeon, an immigrant from Europe. Other dove kinfolk important to hunters are the white-winged dove, or whitewing, and the band-tailed pigeon. Seven states—Arizona, Colorado, New Mexico, Oregon, Utah, Washington, and parts of California—have open hunting seasons for band-tailed pigeons. Arizona, New Mexico, and parts of California, Nevada, and Texas have whitewing seasons.

If you've hunted in the South, you've probably flushed the ground dove, much smaller than the mourning dove, a chestnut color. The ground dove, not a game bird, is protected year-round. This little bird knows it, and that's why you can get so close to it. However, it plays a dangerous game; a hunter catching its silhouette from the corner of his eyes cannot help throwing his gun up. Charley has done the same thing when grasshoppers flush. This always elicits unnecessary remarks from nearby companions—until they do the same thing.

The mourning dove provides the largest harvest of any game bird. Its adaptability has earned it the distinction of being the only game bird which nests in every state but Alaska. Its formal name, *Zenaidura macroura,* which sounds like a girl from a Polynesian island, has an interesting derivation from Zenaide, the wife of a nephew of Napoleon Bonaparte. The second name describes the bird's long tail which is distinctly pointed when closed.

Whitewings and bandtails have blunt-ended tails. The mourning dove has a sort of pea-sized head which looks too small for the body. If you compare doves on the basis of World War II

The white-winged dove is a great favorite of hunters in the Southwest. (Photo credit: Texas Parks and Wildlife Department)

fighter planes, the mourning dove is built like a P-51, and the larger two resemble P-47s. The average mourning dove weighs four to five ounces; sometimes mature adults may weigh less, and once in a while a giant reaches six ounces. The bandtail weighs from 12 to 14 ounces, and the whitewing is about halfway in between. The mourning dove flies a little faster than his larger cousins and puts on more aerobatic demonstrations. All three species tend to migrate the day before the hunting season opens.

The mourning dove is decked out in various shades of brown and gray with black spots on the back and wings. The undersides of the tail feathers are prominently tipped in white with a band of black leading into buff or light gray. Under certain light conditions in the field, the white is a distinguishing feature: when you see it, the dove is not surrendering but just landing or pouring on the coal.

To the casual hunter the male and female look alike. At closer inspection you will notice the male's head has a pale bluish color on the top and back, while the female's head is brown or tan. As with most species of bird life, the male is more brightly colored. His neck feathers have a suggestion of irridescent lavender, pink, or purple mixed with metallic gold and basic brown. The bright colors stretch for about two inches along the neck to the chest but are faint unless sunlight strikes them. The female's neck feathers are usually light brown although once in a while they will have a suggestion of the male's bright sparkles. The doves themselves never have any trouble telling male from female, regardless of color. The sex ratio is about 50-50, always a good idea. It makes everything come out even in the breeding season, and nobody gets frustrated.

The males and females are the same size—about 12 inches long from the bill to the tip of

Mourning doves have sharp, pointed tails. (Photo credit: Florida Game and Fresh Water Fish Commission)

the tail with a wingspread of 12 to 14 inches. They have pointed wing tips which meet underneath the body when the bird is in flight. The wings sometimes give off a whistling noise when the birds are flying by and nearly always when they are flushed. Hunters say this is caused by the sound barrier being broken!

Now, it isn't necessary to know all the details of dove life in order to hunt them successfully, but the more you know about a species, the more enjoyable the sport will become. It takes only one trip to a good dove field to give you a healthy respect for the bird's flying ability. You will appreciate your quarry even more when you understand all that must take place for you to bag just one mourning dove. Since whitewing and bandtail are important in only a few states, they are discussed briefly in parts of following chapters.

The mourning dove nests as far south as Central America (especially in Mexico) and as far north as Southern Canada. Most of the birds in the continental United States migrate in autumn or fall, but some hardier doves spend the winter in latitudes as far north as Indiana and Connecticut. One of Charley's Laws states that the dove is erratic, so it's difficult to make an ironclad statement about it without someone popping up with an exception. For the purposes of this book, we're talking about what happens most of the time.

Doves don't waste any time when they decide to mate. It takes a little over a month for them to build a nest, incubate two eggs, and care for the

Nesting doves lead a busy life feeding and caring for their young, which grow rapidly. (Photo credit: Texas Parks and Wildlife Department)

nestlings. Then they're ready to start all over again. In Florida or South Texas, a pair of doves may bring off six hatches a season. Generally, the farther north they are during the spring and summer months, the fewer hatches they'll have, since daylight hours are an important factor. In Wisconsin or Minnesota, a mated pair will do well to bring off two hatches. If the nest or eggs are destroyed, the birds don't get discouraged but start all over. Because of the dove's high annual mortality rate, it's a good system.

There is some evidence that in southern latitudes an early hatch of birds may produce its own offspring by August or September. When it comes to breeding, doves do all sorts of tricky things. Birds from Nebraska wintering in Mexico may bring off a late winter hatch before they fly back to Nebraska for the scheduled mating season. Birds in the Deep South may start nesting as early as January or February, but the peak period for most of the nation is May and June with breeding generally coming to a halt in August or September.

Most wildlife biologists believe that a pair of doves mate only for a season, not for life. At the end of the mating season, the birds scatter and make up new flocks which may spend the winter at home or move to the lower half of the United States or Mexico. A wife gets a new husband every year in late winter or early spring. The doves wouldn't have it any other way.

On the first springlike days courtship begins with much reciprocal cooing and rubbing of bills. There are few elaborate displays and little strutting around as with birds like the woodcock. Courting continues at intervals throughout the breeding season. During nesting, a dove may return at any time during the day to make love to its partner. They really believe in nooners and matinees and this keeps the divorce rate low, at least for a season.

Mated pairs usually select tree nesting sites in clearings and along the edges of fields, pastures, and orchards. Many are attracted to suburbs and even city parks. The nests are usually built within 12 or 15 feet of the ground, but once in a while a pair will nest 50 or 60 feet high or even on the ground. They do this just to keep wildlife biologists on their toes. Although the dove is not a highly territorial bird, there is seldom more than one nest per tree.

Doves are devoted parents but careless home builders. The nest-making procedure consists of the male bringing twigs, grass, and straw to the female who slaps the pieces together in a tree crotch or on a flat limb fork. The result is generally a flat construction often so flimsy that the eggs can be seen from below. Doves won't travel far for construction materials; they use whatever is handy and take about a week to complete a nest. The really lazy ones use old nests left by mockingbirds, blue jays, or other good home builders.

The female usually lays an egg the first day after the nest is built. The day after, she lays her second and final egg. Now and then a dove will lay three eggs, or another female will come in and deposit her own egg or two. However, each nesting period usually produces only two eggs, and the nestlings are usually of the same sex.

Incubation, a two-week process, starts when the first egg is laid. The second egg, laid a day later, is hatched a day after the first chick. The male is quite good about helping with incubation. He usually sits on the nest from about 8:00 a.m. until late in the afternoon, giving the female time to look for food, water, and grit as well as to complete her preening rites.

At hatching time, the chick pecks a hole in the eggshell with the pip on the end of its bill and cuts through about one-fourth of the shell. It then struggles to get out, and, upon bursting into a new world, lies helplessly in the nest for an hour or so until the white natal down dries.

Nestlings are weak and fairly inactive for a few days except for eating. They double in weight during the first 24 hours and continue growing rapidly until they leave the nest when 11 or 12 days of age. The parents keep feeding them until they're about 21 days old, have learned to find their own food, and have perhaps flocked up with other young doves. They go from egg to

adult responsibility in three weeks and develop no complexes in the process.

The newly hatched birds are fed with "dove milk," a white concentrated curd secreted from glands on both sides of the crop of each parent. The hungry nestlings receive this nutritious food several times a day from the mouths of their parents. The feeding process is about like mouth-to-mouth resuscitation except that the adults pass along milk instead of air. The adults soon mix in various seeds, and in a short time the nestlings are eating mostly seeds as do their parents.

Because the birds grow quickly, the parents have to hustle to supply their energy needs. Pinfeathers begin replacing the natal down when the birds are three days old. At one week of age, they begin to exercise their wings by flapping them. Most of a typical day is spent eating, preening, and just looking around. By the tenth day, they become bold enough to hop from the nest to a nearby branch.

The first test flight is taken on the morning of their eleventh or twelfth day. The bobtail fledglings look too soft and fat to be aerodynamically

White-winged doves, like mourning doves, feed their young by regurgitating "milk." (Photo credit: Texas Parks and Wildlife Department)

Mourning dove loafs in a pine tree.

sound. Fortunately, they are unaware of this and solo with complete confidence. Their first flights are short, and returns to the nest are rewarded with food and praise from the adults. In ten days or so, the nestlings leave home and never come back. Their elders react to this departure by beginning the whole process of parenthood over again.

Birds under five months of age have white-tipped wing feathers, both the long primaries and the coverts over the primaries. By understanding how the long wing feathers are replaced by molting, you can distinguish between young birds (under five months) and older birds.

The mourning dove has 10 primary feathers in each wing. The inside primary is number one and the numbers increase toward the outermost long wing feather. The young bird has white-tipped and sharp-ended feathers; the older bird has solid-colored wing tips with rounder ends.

The number one primary is replaced when the bird is between 30 and 40 days old. The feathers, going from one to 10, are consecutively replaced every 10 to 12 days. If you bag a bird with only the number 10 feather white tipped, it would be roughly 125 to 150 days old. Once all the feathers have molted and been replaced, you can no longer tell age unless the 9 and 10 primaries look new, and then you can make a guess.

Aging is of great value to biologists in their field studies and banding programs. It helps them get a picture of the juvenile-adult age ratio by checking bags in the field. Once a dove is over five or six weeks old, you can't tell in the air if it's a young bird or an old one. If you shoot a young bird, it may weigh as much as an adult.

If you learn to determine the age of birds, to tell whether they're under or over about 150 days, you will generally find that for a season's

The primary (long) feathers of juvenile doves are more pointed than those of adult doves; some or all have white tips. (Photo credit: Florida Game and Fresh Water Fish Commission)

Mature doves have primary (the long ones) feathers which are rounded at the ends with little or no white tip. (Photo credit: Florida Game and Fresh Water Fish Commission)

average about seven out of ten birds in hand are young birds which are not as wary as veterans. A three-year-old dove is regarded as an octogenarian, although there are a few instances of eight-year-old banded birds on record. Also, the annual mortality rate for doves is 65 to 80 percent (whether or not they are hunted) and roughly a 4 to 1 ratio of increase is expected in a year of normal reproduction. Fortunately, any short-lived species has a high reproductive bounce-back, and we have seen that the dove is no exception to this rule.

From a culinary point, some hunters like to divide their doves according to age and separate them for cooking. For instance, the tender younger birds are more suitable for frying than the older ones.

Mother Nature's primary concern is not for the individual but for the survival of the species. Dove mortality begins before the eggs are laid. About 5 percent of the nests are abandoned before any eggs are deposited, if, for example, one of the mated pair dies or changes its mind.

Because doves usually build haphazard nests, it doesn't take much of a wind to blow them loose and splatter the eggs below. The nests, usually located close to the ground for the sake of convenience rather than camouflage, are also easily raided by cats, crows, and jays. Hawks and owls are too smart to pass up such an easy meal and all sorts of predators, like dogs, will pick up a squab blown out of the nest. However, predation is not a limiting factor in the number of doves in the fall. The dove more than compensates for these losses with its amazing reproductive ability. As far as the overall dove population is concerned, any predator control program is a waste of time and money.

Hard rain or freezing weather during the nesting season may increase the death toll, as do external and internal parasites. Doves, especially during high population buildups, are quite susceptible to contagious diseases. One of the worst is trichomoniasis, or canker, which in some cases can thin out flocks over a wide area. Death is caused by starvation as the mouths and throats close up with yellow lumps. Doves also catch fowl pox and other diseases, although researchers do not yet know how adversely these affect the population. A dove's life is not an easy one, though the government tries to look after it.

Massive freezes which keep birds from feeding can prove disastrous. As long as the doves are able to get feed, they can keep their body temperatures up, but if they have to do without nutrition for two or three days in cold weather, they are in big trouble. A body weak from hunger is subject to infection and death.

The biggest predator is man! Yet 3 million gunners scattered across 32 states only account for about 12 or 13 percent of the dove population each hunting season. This includes birds bagged and those knocked down but not recovered.

The sum of the various percentage guesses for mortality doesn't total up to the 65 to 80 percent annual turnover ascertained by biologists. There seems to be a limiting factor, perhaps in the bird itself, which has not yet been discovered by research. If the population gets too high, disease or some other factor steps in to reduce it. If the population dwindles, the birds have the capability of bringing it back in a season or two. Nature, as usual, knows what she's doing even if man doesn't.

Doves don't seem to care what they eat as long as it is in the form of seeds; in fact, about 99 percent of their food is wild seeds or agricultural

Mourning dove nestles close to give warmth to two chicks. (Photo credit: Virginia Commission of Game and Inland Fisheries)

seeds such as corn, peas, grain sorghum, wheat, barley, peanuts, or sunflower.

Mourning doves don't pay as much attention to which food it is as to how easy it is to get. They come pretty close to wanting their food served on silver platters. Doves are not diggers or scratchers—they look for food lying loose on bare ground. Some doves will eat under a bird feeder in the suburbs but refuse to land on the feeder. They'll eat fruit seeds on the ground but rarely take a peck at fruit on trees. They would as soon have weed seeds as farm crops, and if the weed seeds are lying on the ground, they'll take them every time rather than pick at corn hanging on the stalk.

Their eating habits are important to hunters because most shooting in America is done over fields being used by birds for feeding. Doves do not like to land in thick grass or other cover where their vision is restricted. Apparently they want to see what might be approaching. They want their feet on the ground, and so they seek feed which is lying on the top of the soil. For instance, a peanut field worked over by hogs is ideal for them. The cover is down, and whole or pieces of peanuts are easily available on the surface. Most of the time, doves won't work hard to feed; they simply fly until they find easy pickings.

Adult doves usually start feeding at dawn's early light or later if it's cloudy or rainy. Depending upon the availability of feed, they may load their crops in 15 to 20 minutes or spend an hour or two milling about. After they have eaten, they fly to water. Doves and pigeons drink

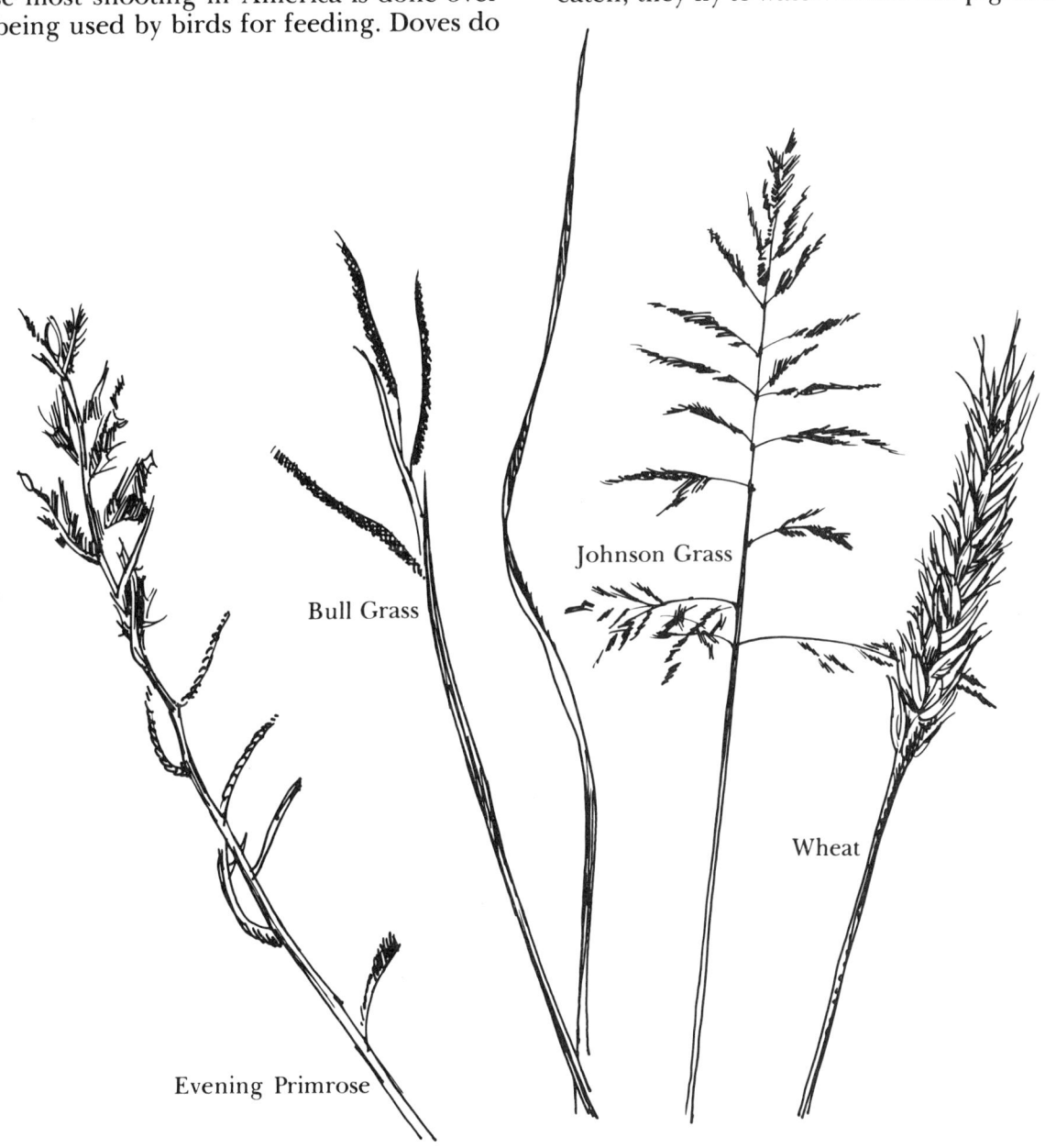

Evening Primrose | Bull Grass | Johnson Grass | Wheat

White-winged doves are colony breeders. They are often found in large concentrations during the hunting season. (Photo credit: Texas Parks and Wildlife Department)

differently from most birds. Instead of taking a bill full and holding their heads back, they dunk their bills and drink until satisfied.

During the middle of the day, the birds sit in trees and loaf, preen their feathers, or pick up grit to aid in grinding food in their gizzards. Sometimes they fly to the ground and dust a few lice off, but most of the time they love to sit in trees and gossip.

Around three or four o'clock in the afternoon, the birds fly to feed again. If the feed is abundant, they'll jam their crops to the bulging point. They fly to water late in the afternoon and then head for tree roosts.

The dove's lifestyle seems to be one of loafing hard and flying hard. It spends five to six hours a day in contented idleness and on necessary flights to food, water, and roosts. It flies wide open—full throttle is its favorite speed.

Mourning doves are social birds. They like company. During the breeding season the adults are quite satisfied with their mates, but in September or October the pairs split up and join any available flock. The young birds just out of the nest quickly become members of any passing flock.

Thousands of doves may congregate around a cattle feedlot where grain is handy. The birds have adapted well to the bounty of modern big-time farming where a percentage of grain is left in the field during harvesting. Large and small flocks work in and out of these free cafeterias, apparently breaking up and rejoining at random. Doves don't seem to care whom they associate with as long as it is other doves.

Flocks vary in number from three to hundreds. Under most hunting conditions you'll be charged by flocks of three to twenty birds, although several thousand doves may be working in and out of a huge feeding field. If you see a lone dove during the hunting season, it's looking for company for dining, loafing, and sleeping purposes.

Because the dove is a migratory bird, its welfare is protected by the Fish and Wildlife Service, a division of the U.S. Department of the Interior, as well as by individual states. For management purposes, the Service divides the central 48 states into three geographical units—Eastern, Central, and Western Management Units. These units correspond very closely to the way doves migrate. For instance, about 95 percent of the birds shot in a geographical unit were hatched somewhere within that same unit.

The migration patterns of doves have not been worked out as definitively as those of waterfowl. One reason is that biologists seldom get more than three or four percent returns on banded doves. However, biologists are as persistent as the birds are erratic, and with the help of state and federal programs, plus computers, the major movements have become fairly well known.

To understand dove migration, you have to forget about the many exceptions and concentrate on what most doves do. The whitewing, for instance, is not normally found east of Texas, but once in a while a Marco Polo is trapped by a biologist in Florida.

There is considerable evidence that young birds flocked together in the northern and middle states may start south in July and August

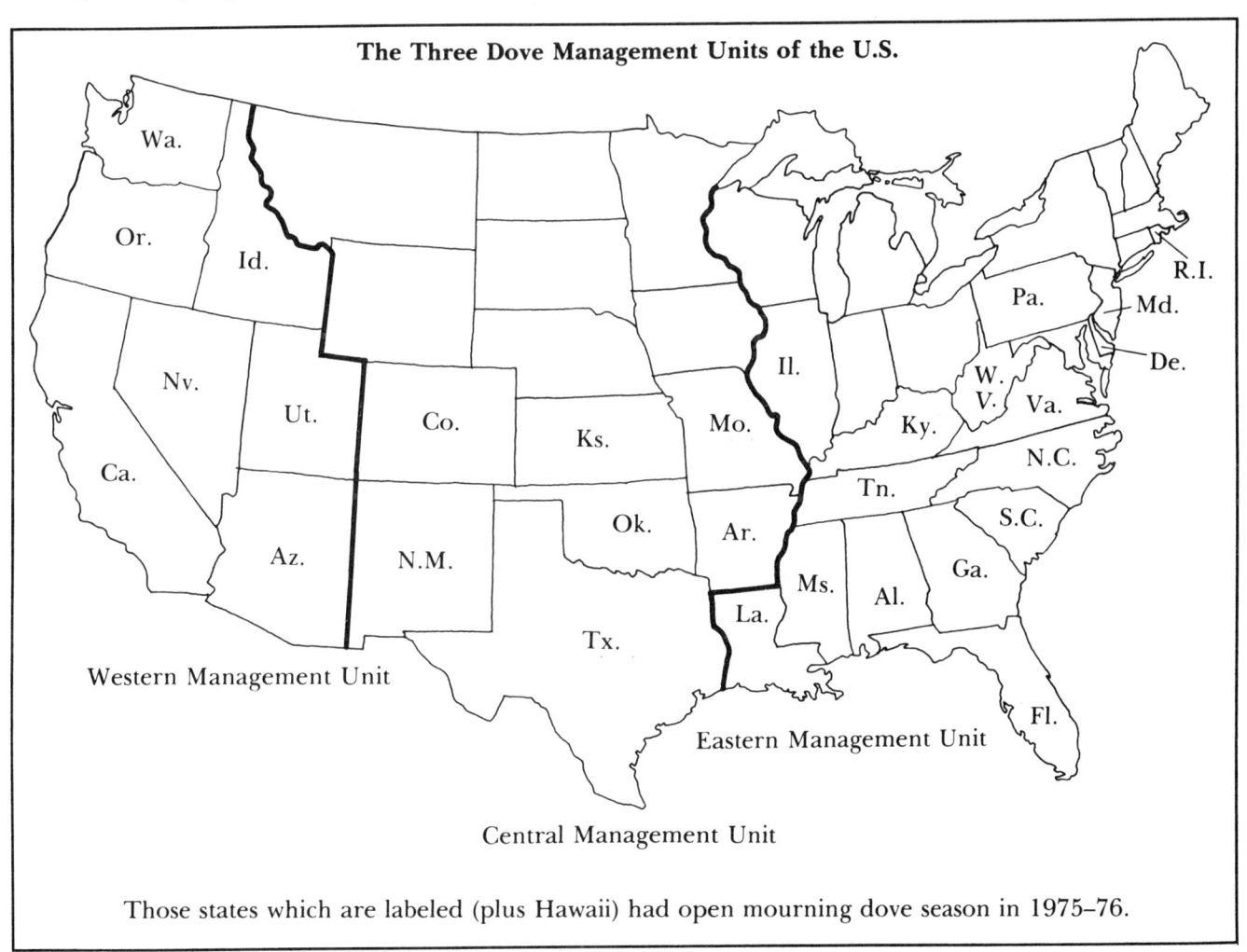

The Three Dove Management Units of the U.S.

Those states which are labeled (plus Hawaii) had open mourning dove season in 1975–76.

when the adults are still trying to bring off another hatch. The parents wait until the last fledglings are independent and then scramble.

Many biologists believe the doves that summer in the north to be a more hearty strain than those that live all their lives in the southern states. There is good reason for this. Some doves stay north all winter and somehow survive, although most move to the warmer climates of the southernmost states, Mexico, and a few move to Cuba.

Cool weather is generally credited with being the trigger that sends doves south for a winter vacation, although there are bound to be other factors involved which are not yet fully understood or defined. There is a strong argument that doves have an instinctive drive to migrate, although the imported ones in Hawaii don't migrate off the islands or they would drown.

A lot of the first migration is similar to leapfrogging. The northern birds migrate to the middle states while the middle-state doves move south. Doves from Cape Cod and Wisconsin may fly to Central Alabama while birds from that area move to South Florida.

In the San Joaquin Valley of California, where daytime temperatures in late August and early September run over 100°, hunters pray that the thermometer won't drop a few degrees. They know from bitter experience that if it does, their rich crop of doves will depart. Later in the season they get a new supply of doves drifting through from Northern California, Washington, and Oregon. What triggers one area of doves to migrate may not set off another bunch. A flock of doves from South Dakota may move to North Texas while the local birds move no farther than South Texas. Doves in North Florida may move south and have their grain fields taken over by birds from Illinois, Indiana, and Kentucky.

Some flocks seem to work their way south in leisurely fashion, since autumn is the time of plenty. Others pick up and move several hundred miles a day. Some unusual band recoveries prove that doves can move 500 miles a day if sufficiently motivated.

The movements are not necessarily in a straight north-south direction but may have an easterly or westerly slant. Why a Missouri dove moves to Southern Alabama rather than making a shorter trip to Southern Louisiana, no one knows but the dove. Why South Georgia doves move to the Florida Keys when doves from Pennsylvania and Maryland find South Georgia an ideal winter home is a mystery.

Perhaps someday all the mystery surrounding dove migration will be explained. You can help hasten that day by checking each dove you bag for a band and returning it to the address shown. The more information biologists acquire, the more accurately they can set seasons for maximum harvest with no danger to the basic breeding flock.

The bulk of the continental dove flock winters in the lower tier of southern states and Mexico. Within this area, it undertakes considerable local moving to find food, water, and shelter. Mortality continues throughout the winter, long after the shooting seasons have closed. In fact, once the peak populations of August and September are reached, the numbers of birds decrease in all ranges regardless of hunting. Sudden cold fronts bringing freezing rain, snow, or ice are disastrous, and disease attacks whenever flocks build up too much. Starvation confronts the doves even in a land of plenty because the bird takes only feed which is easy to get. Despite its adaptability to living with man, it has never learned to dig and scratch for its food.

In late winter and early spring, the remaining doves migrate and spread back across the nation to pair off, mate, and begin another breeding cycle.

It is not necessary for you to be a naturalist to enjoy dove hunting or even to be a great wing shooter. Most of us simply want to know where there are plenty of doves on the day we go hunting. But any hunter who calls himself a true sportsman must have some respect for and understanding of his quarry.

For you to pull your shotgun trigger a single time, your darting, turning target may have flown a thousand miles and lived a hazardous life unthinkable to modern man in his comforts. You owe the dove the respect of taking a shot only when you have a reasonable chance of killing it cleanly and recovering it.

In many respects, the dove is a bird accidentally available for the hunter. Man is not directly responsible for its abundance. The dove has prospered under modern farming conditions and nearly all of man's management pertains to harvest. Charley likes to call it the manna bird—there every autumn and fall for the hunter to take a portion and enjoy—a remarkable, renewable resource.

The mourning dove is the all-American game bird. An unknown writer in South Carolina affectionately described it as "a bird which sings like a nun, walks like a big-chested, little old lady, whistles like a squeaking rusty gate, and flies like a bat out of hell."

Types of Dove Hunting

Dove hunting is not so much actual hunting as it is searching for a place to shoot. Once you locate a flight line or concentration of doves, you can set up, get comfortable, and let the birds come to you. Doves are the easiest of all birds to hunt but the hardest to shoot. For the average hunter to bag 10 or 12 doves, he must shoot at about 60 or 70 which fly into range. To get that many shots, he has to be in an area where the birds are ganged up.

Most hunters are not happy unless they leave the field with a daily limit. To reach this goal, they hunt for an area where doves are concentrated or moving in and out.

Limits and shooting hours vary among the three federal management units. For the 1975-76 hunting season in the Eastern Management Unit, legal shooting hours were from noon until sunset with a daily bag limit of 12 birds and total possession limit of 24 after the first day. In the Central and Western Management Units, legal shooting hours were from 30 minutes before sunrise until sunset except for Texas, where shooting times varied by zone. The daily bag limit was 10 doves with a total possession limit of 20 after the first day.

In any one day a hunter may not take more than one day's limit. If a hunter is on a trip of two days, he can shoot a legal daily limit the first and second days and transport them home. However, it is not a good idea to go into a field the second day with birds shot the first day in your possession. You might have trouble explaining to an unsympathetic federal or state wildlife officer why you have 15 or so birds, and he might well curtail your shooting.

Federal and state regulations are subject to change every year, and it is the hunter's responsibility to know and obey the changes. Law enforcement officers are not noted for accepting alibis, probably because they've heard most of them. I once heard a hunter over the limit piously explain to a state warden that he had shot the extra birds to take to the county poorhouse. The officer replied that if he was that civic minded, he might like to go with him to the county judge and make a monetary contribution. The judge decided that $100.00 would be an appropriate gesture.

Most hunters have a handy supply of clichés about why they like to hunt which they will recite on demand. However highly the beauties of nature and the joys of going afield with old buddies rank among the reasons, an undeniable (if unspoken) thrill is that of being among the first to bag a limit and leave the field early in full view of the other hunters. No one can portray false modesty quite so dramatically as the first hunter to get a limit.

The hunter who leaves a field at sunset with his hard-won daily limit feels much satisfaction. He will sidle over to you and ask how you did. You may as well return the question, for he will finally force you into it. Then he'll nonchalantly reply, "Oh, I limited out."

If the management unit has a limit of 10 doves, it would seem that the hunter who bagged 9 birds would have had at least 9/10 as good a time as the hunter who bagged 10. But it just doesn't work that way. A limit is the goal of nearly all shooters. In fact, when I have returned to the cars at sunset short a bird or two, I have been intimidated enough by the prospect of making my failure public to lie and say that I couldn't find several birds which I had shot the hearts out of.

The most fertile dove hunting grounds in America are grain fields whose seeds are lying temptingly on the bare surface just waiting to be eaten. Doves pour into this paradise, and flock after flock may keep returning despite a barrage of shells. In the southern half of the United States and Mexico, hundreds and even thousands of birds may concentrate in one field to feed. Apparently doves hate to dine alone.

In the large agricultural fields from Eastern Virginia to California, 10 to 50 shooters may surround one field. The shooting is as much a social event as an old-fashioned barbecue supper. The owner of the land, or one of his appointees, watches the dove buildup until there is a large enough concentration to give a lot of shooters more than ample opportunity to bag limits. When the time is right, word travels fast, and there is a gathering of the clan.

The farmer designates stands or actually builds loose blinds in the field. Then the shooters are delivered to the blinds in pickup trucks, and the only exercise anyone gets is craning his neck and walking out to pick up a shot dove. As the doves pour in to feed, everyone blasts away, and this keeps the birds moving. At peak feeding time, there are hundreds of birds flying the gauntlet in and out of the field. Gun barrels smoke with the rapid shooting, and expert wing shooters quickly get a limit as duffers open up

new boxes of shells.

The larger shoots with huge numbers of birds are popular with city hunters, as they promise optimum conditions for bagging limits. The big shootouts are also favored by many landowners. A farmer friend of mine who lives in a remote region of Louisiana has two shoots a season to pay off social obligations and to endear himself to those townspeople he may need favors from during the year. These include a priest, two doctors, members of a law firm, two bankers, a bootlegger, and the manager of a hospital. A dentist, the tax assessor, the parish judge, farm equipment mechanics, and assorted relatives are also invited. They all look forward to the shoots, and the farmer who organizes these hunts receives special attention—free whiskey deliveries, he has never been put in jail, and he has been known to receive house calls from doctors at midnight.

In the big-time farming country there is a practical shooting reason for having a lot of gunners. Three or four hunters in a 200-acre field of harvested milo simply cannot keep the doves moving. The birds land in a corner away from the hunters, quickly fill their crops (especially if they're feeding on something as large as peanuts or corn), and depart for trees or watering spots. This violates a basic principle of dove shooting at a feeding field—keep the birds from feeding. While they are hungry, they may keep making passes over the field. Although there is nothing to prevent them from flying to another field, they are creatures of habit, and if accustomed to feeding in a particular field, they will keep returning to it. It is a common sight, especially on opening day or the early part of the season, to see a dove scoot through a barrage of a dozen gunners, escape undamaged, turn, and come back to try to land in the same field.

There is no surefire way of predicting how much shooting a concentration of doves will accept before deciding to depart. Many who would otherwise return to brave the shells might be deterred by a cold front or a desire for a change in diet.

Ideal hunting tactics, then, for a feeding field are for the shooters to get their limits quickly, leave, and let the birds sit down to feed. The birds are more likely to come back the next day if they are soon able to feed.

One of Charley's Laws states that the larger the group of hunters in a feeding field, the greater the probability that it will be "burned out" in a single day or in one shoot. That is, the doves will finally realize that prolonged shooting is hazardous to their health and will fly off to locate a quieter field. Local birds may not come back to feed for a week or longer, if at all, although birds migrating into the area may use it.

There is nothing mysterious about this "burning out" principle—experienced hunters and farmers know it well. Some farmers whose land is loaded with doves may not let you on their land because they say you will spook the doves and spoil their plans for a big shoot. This simply may be a polite way of refusing you permission to hunt. Other farmers, who like to hunt and invite many people, prefer to have one or two huge shootouts rather than a series of small hunts.

At times, other hunters can be an advantage to you. If the birds are not coming to your field, shooting may start up in other fields and push them your way. I have often bagged a limit by stationing myself in some woods between two fields being hunted and taking the passing shots as birds zipped back and forth trying to find a safe place to feed.

You must scout doves yourself unless several good hunting friends are willing to share the findings of their efforts with you. If you are looking for feeding (and flying) doves, you must track them during the two major feeding periods—early morning and late afternoon. This is when they are most active. At other times you may drive miles and miles through heavily populated dove country and never see a flash of feather except perhaps on a telephone wire. Remember, in the heat of the day they are contentedly loafing in scrub or sitting in trees, and they are not easily visible.

If the management unit you are located in has morning shooting, you should be scouting at daybreak. If shooting starts at noon, you should be in the field looking at about 3:00 p.m., which may be a little early under average conditions. The afternoon movement varies a lot according to the weather, distance to feeding grounds, hunting pressure, and other factors known only to the doves themselves.

On a given afternoon you may see one concentration of doves in a milo field, another a mile away eating corn, and a third flock eating grass seeds such as lespedeza. Why aren't they all in the corn field or all in the milo field? I don't have the answer and neither do the biologists. Apparently doves like variety in their menus, but accessibility is a more primary concern than the kind of food they eat. To reemphasize an earlier observation, they are not diggers and scratchers.

They want their seeds lying on the ground, preferably bare ground. They want to eat in the open and do not like to fly into ground cover. When they land, they like to be able to see a great distance at their eye level.

This means that most of the time they feed in harvested fields of grain where the stalks are knocked down or where there is low stubble. If weed stalks have been knocked down or disked, doves will readily feed on weed seeds. If grasses have been mowed or grazed down, they will gladly accept grass seeds. There are exceptions, of course, but open or bare ground with sparse or no cover is what they prefer. The Western mourning dove somehow manages to scratch a living out of his desert or semiarid surroundings but is probably much happier to move into irrigated farm country or feedlots in the autumn.

By understanding the conditions doves generally expect for feeding, you can automatically eliminate a lot of territory inappropriate for hunting as you drive through the countryside looking for flocks. In some wheat states, there may be mile after mile of nothing but wheat fields. The doves will choose some and pass up others, although the fields may look alike to you. When scouting under these conditions, you simply stop the car to see which field they're using and, depending on the time of day, get permission from the farmer to hunt then or come back the next day. Chances are good that the doves will be in the same field the next day, although you cannot be certain. Doves, not given to much planning ahead, don't really care where they are the next day or the next week.

Doves often concentrate near the huge grain silos of the Midwest and the large cattle feedlots of the Mid- and Southwest. In both operations grain is inadvertently spilled on the ground and quickly located by doves and rock pigeons. Naturally, the feedlot operators do not want you to scare the cattle by shooting near them. However, you may be able to enjoy pass shooting 300 or 400 yards away without disturbing the cattle.

The most popular time for dove shooting in America is when the birds are entering or leaving a feeding area. It is against federal regulations to bait migratory birds for the purpose of shooting, but it is legal to shoot in those areas where feed on the ground is a part of normal farming operation. Furthermore, it is legal to plant feed to attract doves to the gun (recently this law was liberalized to allow the grain to be cut or knocked down), but it is illegal to harvest the seed and scatter it somewhere else.

The regulations on shooting over feed are fairly complicated and may change from time to time. Free copies of the regulations are available from the various regional offices of the U.S. Fish and Wildlife Service listed in the Appendix.

When in doubt about the legality of shooting in a particular feeding field, a good maxim is Don't! If you have the time and the landowner's permission, you may want to fetch a wildlife officer to look the situation over and give you a ruling.

If you are not careful, you may innocently violate the regulations. Years ago, when shooting in Georgia started at daylight, a generous farmer had invited a group of about 35 hunters to shoot on his land. We were at our stands before dawn, and when the sun tipped the horizon hundreds of doves zoomed in on us. I finally knocked down a darting dove and hurried into the disked corn field to retrieve it.

As I searched for my bird in the expanding light, it occurred to me that I was trampling over strange corn stalks—they produced both white and yellow corn! When I looked closer, I saw splatters of milo on the ground mixed with millet. The farmer, anxious that we have plenty of targets, had "sweetened" the field with extra grain. I grabbed my gear, stopped by the farmer's blind, and told him that I'd had too much branch water the night before, and I'd see him at his home for breakfast. The shoot was not raided, but if it had been the Feds would have hit the jackpot!

The next most popular method of shooting doves is to wait for them at a watering spot or on a flight line not far from the water. Normally, doves fly to water after the early morning feeding period and again following the late afternoon snack. Where water is scarce, they do not mind flying 5 or 10 miles to dip their bills and suck in the refreshing liquid.

The morning drink is often more leisurely than the one in late afternoon. After the morning feed, they have 6 or more hours of loafing ahead of them and may hang around the pond for a while, sometimes picking up grit or simply preening.

The afternoon drink is usually during the last hour before dark. Generally, the birds fly in, land close to the water, and waddle down and dunk their bills. When they are saturated, they fly from the water toward their roost.

The dove prefers an open landing spot near water. He wants to light where he can see for a considerable distance at his eye level. He likes his feet on the ground. He will pass up a pond,

Doves flying to water provide sporty shooting.

irrigation canal, or river where the banks are solidly grown up in thick vegetation.

In the Southwest and other arid sections of the country, birds gather at available water in large numbers. Under these conditions, the shooting may be hotter than in a feeding field. Isolated cattle-watering troughs attract doves and whitewings by the thousands. In the Southeast, where there are farm ponds and flowing creeks nearly everywhere, a simple way of attracting doves is to plow or disc a landing strip on the edge of the water. The birds like bare banks, whether in an irrigated desert or in high rainfall country of the East.

One of the best shooting spots I've ever hunted was a small pond in Southeast Alabama. The farmer planted a collar of brown-top millet around the pond which was in turn surrounded by a variety of trees. Brown-top weathers down quickly and the farmer helped it along by dropping the water level to leave a bare landing strip between the feed and water.

Local doves quickly found they liked the convenience of feed and water together. Just the farmer and I hunted the pond, and because he didn't put on any large shoots the area was never burned out, and we enjoyed it frequently for an entire season.

We'd usually go to the pond about three hours before dark to catch the early feeders and move around among the trees until we picked up the direction that the doves would dribble in from. Although the entire water and feed area was only about eight acres, the birds which got by us or came in from the other side would often land and start feeding.

As soon as we had limited out, we'd leave to let the doves feed and drink. On days when we went out late to catch birds moving to water, whether we were filled out or not we'd quit shooting in time for them to drink. As local birds migrated south, others moved in until the shooting closed in December. It was inexpensive to plant the millet, but most of the management was directed toward not overshooting. It paid off with an entire season of successful hunting.

When you are shooting birds which are going to water, it's good management to set up 100 yards or so from the water. On a given day most of the birds will be arriving from one or two main directions and you can maneuver around until you're underneath the flight line. It's also more sporting shooting, because the birds will be flying faster than when circling the pond or trying to land.

One of Charley's Principles states that more than two hunters in a field are unmanageable; four hunters are a swarm and over five are a rambling horde. Ideal shooting stations (at least from the doves' point of view) would be at some distance from the water so that birds which got past the guns could go ahead and drink. Admittedly, this seldom works where there are a lot of hunters. No matter where the hunters set up initially, most will wind up shooting at the pond where the birds are trying to land.

This maneuver is understandable, since many hunters are there for just one shoot and probably are not able to make many hunts in a season. Everyone wants to bag his limit. Besides, the dove is migratory and may be gone tomorrow anyway.

All this means that when you happen upon a watering area with heavy dove traffic, you are faced with two choices. You can take a large number of hunters in for a shoot and risk driving the doves off for a few days or for the remainder of the season, or you can hunt rather judiciously with one or two buddies and come back for many more hunts.

Doves like to sleep together. They don't much care what sort of tree they roost in as long as it offers protection from ground and flying predators. They'll take anything handy from mesquite or cedar to live oak trees for a roost. This brings us to the third most popular way of shooting doves. If you can locate a flight line leading to a roost, you're in for some fast pass shooting as the doves zoom homeward. The shooting may last 15 to 45 minutes before closing time at sunset. Since the time of sunset changes each day, the time you must stop shooting changes every afternoon.

Incidentally, it's important that you wear a watch with an accurate setting when shooting near sunset. In the excitement of the concentrated shooting, it's easy to keep busting caps after the legal closing time. If you fire one shot after closing, you are fair game for a wildlife officer—it doesn't matter whether you hit the dove or not.

By scouting and watching the general directional trend of doves following the afternoon watering period, you can locate roosting areas or the roosts themselves. Depending on a variety of factors such as how many birds are in the area, a particular roost may house anywhere from a score of birds to several hundred. A roost may be a clump of live oaks or an area covering several acres.

In most parts of the nation, doves have a wide range of roosting sites each afternoon. They are

Doves flying into roosting areas late in the afternoon provide top shooting.

not too choosy about what kind of tree they pick and don't seem to mind flying several miles to a roost. From the hunter's standpoint, this means the doves will take only so much pounding before moving to another roosting site where they will not be annoyed.

The farther you shoot from the roost, the better your chances are of the entire flock not skipping out. Of course, the farther you set up from the roost, the harder it is to get directly under the varying flight line each afternoon. At a distance from the roost, the doves come barreling across the treetops and you get only quick passing shots, the most sporting of all shooting.

If you move in to the edge of the roost itself, you'll get circling, diving, landing, and passing shooting with many of the birds below the treetops. You may have no more than 15 minutes of legal shooting, but that may be more than enough time. If there is a concentration of doves, your main problem will be how quickly you can reload your shotgun. However, by moving into the roost you may drive the birds away, and that could be your last shot at the roost for the season.

There are usually wooded islands in the reservoirs built by the TVA, the Army Corps of Engineers, and private power companies. These islands provide ideal roosting conditions, and the doves soon find them.

From the mainland I have shot the flight lines leading to islands in many states, especially Tennessee. Once the doves come under shooting pressure, the flight lines vary each afternoon. It takes a lot of maneuvering to get under the lines, but barrel-burning action is your reward for finding the right spot.

As long as the roosting island itself is not hammered, the birds keep going back. They quickly adjust to danger on the mainland by varying their flight patterns and shying away from the sounds of shooting. Under these conditions, there may be good shooting for many days; but sooner or later a party of hunters will take a boat to the island and burn it out, and you'll have to start scouting again. If you're an experienced hunter, you will have anticipated this and already located other hot spots.

If you're a dove hunter, you can't drive through the countryside without looking for doves. I once drove from Knoxville to Chattanooga with an old-time dove hunter. The way he almost collided with cars and trucks made me think he was loosing his eyesight. I was cringing and stomping out the floorboard until I realized what he was doing. I finally told him that if he'd look at the highway, I'd count the doves.

That evening at dinner, following several liquid appetizers, he grinningly exhibited the recall of his photographic memory. Starting with the salad and ending with dessert, he told me exactly where every dove along the 100-mile drive had been spotted. He told me whether they had been in walnut trees or on telephone lines. He remembered each dove which had been flying and its altitude and direction. I was so amazed by this display that I would not have been surprised had he told me what the doves were saying to one another.

As he sensed my appreciation for his perfor-

Mourning Dove

mance, he became quite expansive and told me how he'd trained himself in the art of observing and remembering doves over the years—much like a bridge player who the next day can remember each hand and who held what. Finally, I was unable to resist putting this lovable old codger to the test.

"Lee," I asked, "what color are your wife's eyes?"

"Why," he stammered, "they're blue, no gray, uh . . ."

"Are you sure they're not hazel?"

"Well, they may be sort of brown. . . ."

He broke into a wide smile and said, "If you ever tell May about this, I'll fill you full of dove shot."

If you enjoy dove hunting, the chances are you'll become a dove watcher year-round—whether or not the hunting season is open. My biggest problem is that it causes me to drive past the thruway exits I'm supposed to take.

A fourth method of taking doves is called jump shooting which involves walking and flushing birds from the ground. To get within shooting range, you have to use cover to hide your approach. Most of the doves will flush out of range, and you'll nearly always hear the characteristic whistle when they go up. In fact, this sound may be your first warning that a dove has flushed.

Despite what I've told you about doves preferring to land on bare ground, some will go into corn fields searching for weed seeds. They are unable to see you approaching and flush because they hear you.

It's difficult to get closer than 30 yards to a dove without having it flush. If you're in tall corn, it will take an instant to see the bird. You have to mount your shotgun in a hurry or the bird will be gone.

To walk within range, there must be cover between you and the dove. You can use a fencerow as cover, walk quietly, and hope to put up a bird in range on the other side. Of course, while you are walking and flushing birds some may circle back and fly within range, especially young birds at the first of the season. Also, birds passing over from other areas may fly toward you.

During the middle of the day, the birds loaf in trees. One or two hunters slipping quietly along may be able to jump the birds within range, but most of the birds will spook well ahead of you. For the ones which do jump into range, you have to be fast, because you have about one second to shoot before the bird is out of range.

I've had my best luck jumping birds out of trees by sneaking through mesquite trees in California. The ground is bare between the clumps and walking quietly is easier. Mesquite trees are not high and sometimes doves fly over the tops making themselves clear targets; even so, you must flush many doves to get within clean killing distance of one. Jump shooting is one of the most sporting ways of hunting doves, but not many hunters do it. It's easier to sit comfortably on a stool and try for a limit at a feeding field, water hole, or roost.

On their migratory routes, doves sometimes concentrate at a staging point before moving on. Day after day new birds will arrive, spend the night, and fly south. The doves hit the resting or staging area about the same time every year.

Alligator Point in Florida's panhandle is a famous stopping-off place for doves before they move to central or southern Florida. If you can locate such a staging area on land open to the public, you'll find excellent shooting. Most of it is pass shooting as the birds mill around before taking another leg on their flight to winter headquarters.

Doves are where they want to be, not necessarily where you'd like them to be. For each of 20 to 40 hunters on a social shoot to get his limit, a lot of birds have to be concentrated. They usually are, or else the host wouldn't invite so many guests. However, I still find that hunting with one companion is more enjoyable. Naturally, there must be some birds around, but a large concentration is not needed.

Still hunting, similar to still hunting for deer, is walking, sitting, and watching, and then moving again. It's idly puttering about with a shotgun. Perhaps you try to jump some doves from a loafing area in the woods or from a cornfield. Maybe you can see a few birds flying across in a forming pattern. You find a hiding place under the flight line, put up a few decoys, and wait.

You see doves landing in a small field to feed, and you get on one side and your partner on the other. When they quit coming in, you go to a water hole and sit and wait. Later, when the doves move on, you try to pick up a flight line leading to a small roost.

At some stops you get only a few shots, but at others you do better. After three or four hours, you've probably gotten a lot of chances whether or not you take home a full bag. You've had a pleasant, relaxing afternoon and feel like you've been hunting rather than shooting. I don't find many people who like to hunt doves this way. They'll walk all day for quail or deer, but when it comes to doves they don't want to walk further than from the car to a blind. Anyway, my old dog is always ready to still hunt with me.

Whitewings and Bandtails

Hunting white-winged doves involves about the same techniques as hunting mourning doves, and the two are frequently found together. Whitewings concentrate at feeding fields, feedlots, watering spots, and roosting areas. So do the hunters. Most of the shooting is in early September, before the whitewings take off for Mexico where they become *palomas blancas.*

The band-tailed pigeon feeds mainly on acorns, pinions, and other mast crops. They are mostly found in wooded mountains but sometimes move into farmland when the mast crop is short. Most of the hunting is pass shooting as the birds move over trees looking for acorns and other mast.

Now that we've discussed the various types of shooting, let's talk about hunting for a *place* to shoot.

Band-tailed Pigeon

Whitewing

White-winged dove protecting and caring for its young. (Photo credit: Texas Parks and Wildlife Department)

White-winged fledglings grow so rapidly you can almost see them expanding. (Photo credit: Texas Parks and Wildlife Department)

A Place to Hunt

The best places to hunt doves are in feeding fields (agricultural land where farmers grow cereals, legumes, grass, and other seeds, plus weed seeds), which are, of course, privately owned.

Although the public owns the game, the farmer controls access to the birds on his property by refusing or granting you permission to shoot on his land. Because a farmer's generosity and goodwill help determine how much dove shooting goes on, it logically follows that sportsmen must do everything possible to get along with farmers and keep them happy.

The farmer is under no obligation to let you on his land. You and I, however, are under the obligation to conduct ourselves in all dealings with farmers in a manner which will favorably reflect on the entire fraternity of hunters.

As every hunter knows, it seems to get a little tougher each year for an urban or suburban hunter to get permission to hunt on farms and ranches. This is not the fault of farmers but mostly the fault of past hunters who did not behave in gentlemanly fashion.

From a practical standpoint, then, each hunter must somehow find several farms which will grant him access to hunt. When he does hunt, his behavior should be exemplary so that he will be welcomed back by his host for years to come.

Millions and millions of words have been written on farmer-sportsman relationships, much of it by state game and fish commissions. What I can't understand is that although I've been hunting for 40 years, from coast to coast, I've never met a single hunter who admitted that he was the one who caused any trouble with farmers. It's always the other guy! Someday before I go to that great game preserve in the sky, I'd like to meet one of those hell-raisers.

The best way to break the ice with farmers you don't know is to drive out and see them before the dove season opens. They are more inclined to grant you permission before the season than in the middle of it. Introduce yourself, hand them a personal card, and say that you'd like to hunt doves on their farms and will abide by any house rules. Also add that you'll never hunt without first checking with them.

One reason that I generally hunt with only one other hunter is that a farmer may not object to two of us coming on his land, but he tends to change his mind when three or four carloads of hunters drive up.

If a farmer grants you permission, write him a thank-you note when you get home that evening, partly because it's the courteous thing to do and partly because it will help him remember you. As the opening day of the season approaches, telephone him, remind him of his promise, and ask if you can come out on such and such a day.

There are about 18 million hunters in America, and roughly 3 million of them hunt doves. That's a lot of traffic. I think farmer-sportsmen relations have generally passed the point where all the hunter had to do was be a jolly good fellow and close the gates. The time has arrived when the sportsman has to do something for the farmer. Why should the farmer be on the giving end all of the time and never on the receiving end?

Doing something for a farmer doesn't necessarily mean writing him a check. Upon seeing my camera, a farmer once asked how much I'd charge to come back on Sunday and make pictures of his deer hounds. I told him I'd be delighted to do it for free.

When I returned, the hounds were scrubbed and brushed. They were as handsome a pack as I'd ever seen, and we spent two hours posing and photographing them. Seeking to endear myself to the whole family, I insisted that we also make pictures of his wife and kids.

He wasn't very enthusiastic about the idea, but he finally consented. It took an hour for the wife to wash and dress the youngsters and get herself ready. She even made the old man put on a tie; he was gone so long I suspected he had trouble finding one.

Anyway, I cranked off several rolls of color and later sent them a batch of prints. It was January before I got back to the farm for quail hunting. The farmer greeted me warmly and guided me into the living room. The place of honor over the fireplace had four beautifully framed hound prints.

To this day, I don't know what happened to the family pictures. They sure weren't on display anywhere I looked. Maybe the family figured that if Pap was happy, they was happy. Anyway, they still let me hunt, and maybe this season I can photograph some new puppies.

These days it takes about a quarter of a million dollars' investment to operate a one-hoss farm. The farmer may not be as interested in payment from hunters as in meeting some nice city folk and making sincere friends. The mere fact that a hunter offers to do something for a farmer is often enough to start a friendly relationship. The very least you can do after a hunt is offer to share your game. The farmer will rarely accept, but he'll appreciate your asking.

I once asked a farmer in a remote area if I could run any errands in town for him. He said he didn't think so; then he paused for a second and said, "You know, I was across the waters during the war. They had dark bread in Europe, and I sure would like to try some again. Reckon you could find any?"

I told him I'd see what I could do. I understood his problem perfectly. The country and small town stores in his area sold only "light" bread, meaning store-bought, wasp's nest, white bread.

This was an easy order to fill. Every time before leaving for his farm, I'd stop by my favorite Jewish delicatessen and buy several loaves of rye, whole wheat, and pumpernickel for my friend. In fact, he got to dropping me post cards wanting to know when I was coming out to hunt again.

But enough! This is a book on dove hunting and not human relationships—a subject without end. If you want to hunt on private lands badly enough, you will develop your own ways of breaking the ice with farmers and getting to know them. You have to make the effort, though—I've never yet had a strange farmer drive up to my suburban home and ask me out to hunt his place!

Some farmers do prefer to be paid and may plant special crops to attract doves, in addition to disking or mowing their fields. There are two general types of operations. One is open to the public, and any hunter who drops in can hunt for a daily fee. The other involves a group or club which leases shooting privileges for the season.

The number of day-shooting farms around the nation is increasing—especially those within easy driving distance of large urban centers where hunters are more willing to pay. Some farmers do no more than simply harvest their fields while others may plant special crops whose seeds will stay on the ground longer than others without decaying. Some of the farmers build

After getting permission from a farmer to hunt, Fred Moses and author look for a hot spot in cornfield.

blinds, or at least camouflage stands, and haul the hunters from the farmhouse to the shooting field. The more convivial farmers even serve hot coffee or cool drinks while the hunters are shooting.

There is no way a farmer can guarantee how much dove shooting you'll get for your money. Doves may decide to go elsewhere at any time. Fees are not standard, but usually range from $5.00 to $10.00 per day. The farmers don't make enough to do much or any advertising. You'll find out about these places through hunting buddies, from sporting goods stores, or by calling your local wildlife officer.

Variations of day-shooting are sometimes conducted by groups of farmers with the proceeds contributed to a community project. Many farmers in Utah give the hunting fees they collect to the Mormon church. I once shot on a ranch in Idaho which belonged to an orphanage, and each hunter contributed what he wanted to.

There is no end to the variations of leasing arrangements. Two hunters may lease one farm, or a shooting club with many members may lease a block of several farms or scattered farms. There is no standard leasing fee, and it's mainly horse trading, perhaps affected by what other farmers in the area are charging.

In the majority of leases, the farmer does no more than conduct his farming in his regular manner. The hunters know that the farm has attracted doves for several years and gamble on its continuing to do so.

In most of the farming area east of the Rockies, it may not pay to plant extra feed to pull doves onto a lease. Farming these days costs too much money, and clubs can't afford to plant enough to compete with nearby fields which are part of other farmers' normal operations.

For arid sections of the West, if a club can get enough irrigation water to plant a field away from big-time farming, it may be a good gamble. It might be cheaper to construct a small pond to attract birds looking for water.

It is risky to spend a great deal of money on development because not even the biologists can predict the results. However, they can make a better guess than sportsmen. In some states, you can get free advice from fish and game departments or the U.S. Soil Conservation Service before spending a lot to build water holes or plant feed.

Roughly two-thirds of the United States is privately owned, and the government owns the other third. Much of the public land is open to outdoor recreation. The urban hunter who does not have access to private land has no choice but to use government land. In America's transient society, with the typical family moving every five years, a lot of people are always searching for a place to hunt.

If you're looking for public land, the best place to start is with your state game and fish department or commission. The addresses of the departments in the 32 states where dove hunting is allowed are listed in the Appendix. If you are new to a state, you may wish to write the department for brochures or publications on dove populations during the hunting season. If

you ask, a department's game management section may send you information on what counties have the best populations. However, they cannot direct you to a particular farm or ranch because only the owner or manager may grant or refuse permission to hunt.

A few state departments own land. Pennsylvania, for example, has over one million acres of land purchased with funds from hunting license sales. Most of the Southern states have a wildlife management area program (WMA) which manages for hunting the lands of private companies in the forest products industry, military reservations, U.S. Forest Service land, and other tracts from the private or governmental sector. Florida, with nearly 5 million acres, is the leading state in the WMA program.

Some states such as North Carolina plant for doves and hold public shoots. Some states operate on a first-come, first-served basis and others by lottery. The amount of planting on WMAs varies by tract and by state. Much of it is essentially woodland and is managed for deer, turkey, squirrels, and other wildlife dependent on forests for survival. WMA land is seldom prime dove country, but areas of it do offer fair dove shooting, especially those which border on agricultural fields. And it has the advantage of being open to the public, usually with the purchase of a permit.

When you contact a state game department, be as specific in your requests for information as you can. Don't, for instance, write a letter and say, "Please send me all the information you have on dove shooting in Kentucky." The state is 500 miles long. The department has a library full of information, but they can't afford to send you copies of everything.

You will get a better and speedier response if you write, "Please send me any handy publications on dove shooting which you now have in print. I live at Bug Tussle and would be willing to drive 100 miles in any direction for the chance to hunt doves. Would you please send me information and maps of any public land in that radius on which I might hunt? Also, please include a copy of the hunting regulations."

The state game departments are doing what they can to provide for public hunting within their limited budgets. However, they cannot afford to buy and maintain farm land at $500 to $1,000 an acre when the hunter pays only $5.00 or $10.00 for a hunting license. One acre of farmland simply does not produce or attract that much wildlife.

Western hunters have access to tremendous acreage administered by the Bureau of Land Management. This agency controls over 400 million acres of land (60 percent of all federal land), most of it in the West and Alaska. Partly because of budget problems with Congress, BLM spends only a penny an acre for fish and wildlife management.

BLM lands are not leased for plant farming, although some is leased for livestock. Doves using BLM lands must feed on native seeds, but

sometimes BLM land is next to farmland where cereal and other dove foods are grown. Doves nest on the lands and use some of the 5 million acres of lakes and reservoirs, plus some of the 259,000 miles of streams, as a welcome source of water. White-winged doves and band-tailed pigeons also use BLM lands.

Much BLM land offers little or no dove shooting, but some of it does provide good hunting, and it is open to the public. The agency has good maps, and the hunter who doesn't mind scouting will find some shooting. Check the Appendix for the addresses of BLM headquarters in various western states.

Parts of some of the National Wildlife Refuges provide dove shooting for the public. The feed planted on land for waterfowl is used by doves; the doves also fly to the refuges to drink and roost. For a list of the refuges which may be open in your section, write the regional headquarters of the U.S. Fish and Wildlife Service for your state as listed in the Appendix.

Doves use the borders and islands in reservoirs of the TVA, Army Corps of Engineers, private power companies, and other water projects. Before using a particular lake, however, make sure that it is open to the public for hunting.

Your state game and fish department has cooperative agreements or a liaison with federal agencies, private power companies, and other large land holders. It will pay you to visit the headquarters or one of the regional offices of your state's department and talk with information specialists about places to hunt. If you're not conveniently located near one of these offices, by all means check with your local wildlife officer. He'll gladly give you some tips.

If you are new to an area, the best way to meet other hunters is to join a local sportsmen's club. The old-timers may give you helpful suggestions on scouting for a place to hunt; sportsmen are not as secretive about migrating dove as they are about resident game.

If you really want to go dove hunting, you can find a place!

Imperial Valley

One of the most unique mourning dove and whitewing hunting areas in America is the Imperial Valley of Southern California. Located just north of the Mexican border, it is more than 100 feet below sea level. Where irrigation canals flow, the desert is changed into rich farm land which produces lush crops year round.

It's a happy breeding ground for doves, and thousands of them concentrate in the grain fields and cattle feedlots. But what makes the valley so unique is that the towns of El Centro, Calexico, Brawley, Holtville, Imperial and others all WELCOME HUNTERS. For the opening of the season, thousands of sportsmen from San Diego to Los Angeles drive to this dove-shooting paradise.

Civic club members from the valley towns work with the farmers to keep their lands open for hunters. The club members draw up maps for the hunters showing the locations of open farms. Parades are held in El Centro, and Calexico even elects a dove queen!

Big banners saying "Welcome, hunters" are strung across the streets. Nearly every store window has a welcome sign. The newspapers run special articles to help the hunters and are filled with ads of welcome. The same is done by the broadcasters who keep the air waves filled with hospitality and hunting hints.

Visiting sportsmen are cheerfully greeted by people on the street, and the restaurants and bars have all sorts of specials to attract them. Several years ago when I hunted the valley with Robert Fuller, television and movie star, we had motel reservations for one carload of hunters, but a second car of Bob's friends joined us. There wasn't a motel room left in town, but one of the hospitality committees got the extra hunters into a Catholic convalescent home. Needless to say, they spent a quieter evening than we did and shot better the next day!

The whole valley works together to make the grand opening a big, friendly hunt every season. The local citizens make a festival of it, and the hunters spend an estimated one million dollars. That's pure gravy—money that would not otherwise come into Imperial County.

It's a rare hunter who doesn't get his limit. The hunters love the hospitality, and the valley folk make a lot of friends and appreciate the income. It's a program hunters wish other counties would copy!

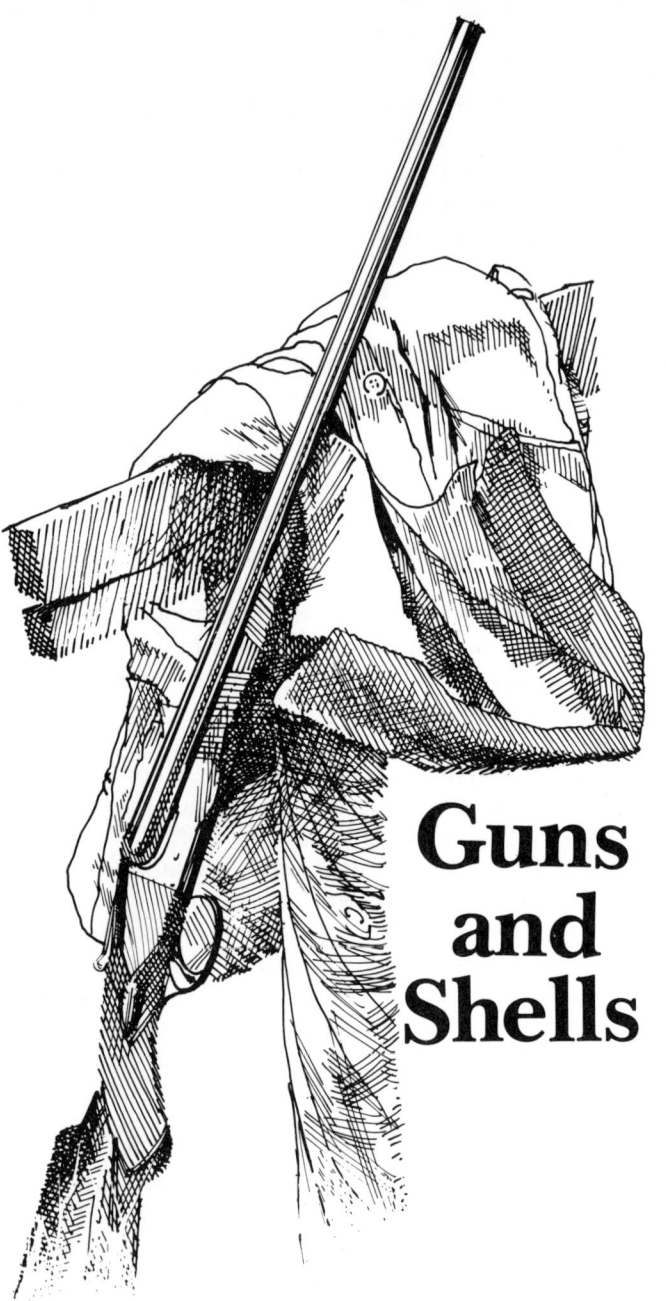

Guns and Shells

You can enjoy dove shooting more cheaply than most other kinds of wing shooting. It takes very little to get started. Assuming you have some old clothes, the only other absolutely essential equipment is a shotgun and shells. If you already own a shotgun, it may be suitable for doves.

There are only four basic types of shotguns. Two of them are called "doubles." Each has two barrels, normally choked differently. One is known as a "side-by-side" double and the other has stacked barrels and is called an "over-and-under."

A third type is the "autoloading" or "semiautomatic," commonly called "automatic," with the ejection and loading cycle handled automatically by the gun's mechanism after firing. The trigger must be pulled for each shot. A true automatic fires continuously with a single pull of the trigger.

The fourth type is called a "pump" or "repeater" or "slide action" shotgun. It is operated manually by pumping or shucking after firing to eject the spent shell from the chamber and move another shell from the magazine to the chamber for firing. A real pump artist can fire three shells faster than the cycle of a semiautomatic will allow.

The semiautomatic and the pump have the advantage of a shell capacity of three or more, as compared to a double which holds only two shells. There are many times in dove shooting when you have time to get off three shots—either on a bird you missed the first two times or on a flock which is bearing down on you. The greatest achievement in dove shooting is to bag a triple. Obviously, you cannot do this with a double-barreled shotgun.

A triple is not getting three birds with one shot; it means knocking down three birds in three successive shots with one continuous movement and no break or pause in the action. It doesn't count as a triple if you knock down two straight and ten minutes later bag another. However, I have seen some great claimers in the field, and I am no longer surprised at anything shooters profess.

One of Charley's Principles on dove shooting is that if you're going to lie, be sure you do all your shooting out of sight of talkative witnesses. Another principle is not to brag on the way to a dove field; if you do, you will surely have a bad day in front of the people you bragged to. If you are lucky and have an outstanding day, let a witness report it to your hunting party. You will garner more glory and be praised for your unassuming manner.

Many semiautomatic and pump shotguns are manufactured to hold more than three shells. For dove hunting, it is illegal for a shotgun to have a capacity of more than three shells—one in the chamber and two in the magazine. It is the shooter's responsibility to make sure that a magazine capable of holding more than two shells is plugged so that no more than two can be inserted.

The federal regulations state, "No person shall take migratory game birds with a shotgun of any description capable of holding more than three shells, unless it is plugged with a one-piece filler, incapable of removal without disassembling the gun, so its total capacity does not exceed three shells." This is one of the first things state and federal wildlife officers check when they convene on you in a dove field.

The most popular semiautomatic shotguns manufactured today are gas-operated. Without getting into technicalitites, this means the gas-operated action reduces recoil from a kick to a nudge. The gas-operated semiautomatic has less recoil than a pump shotgun or the two types of doubles, even if recoil pads are installed on the latter three. Excessive kick not only interferes with the pleasure of shooting but may cause a shooter to start flinching. If a shooter flinches just as he pulls the trigger, his accuracy will go to pot.

In the excitement of shooting at swiftly moving doves, a hunter often fires his shotgun with the butt of the stock everywhere except where it should be, in the V of the shoulder. I've come home with bruises on my lower right bicep and way down my chest, red and blue testimony that I was too excited to mount my gun correctly. If you shoot 50 or 60 shells in a couple of hours, you can take quite a pounding from gun kick and leave the field with a headache.

My right shoulder, then prefers the gas-operated semiautomatic because the kick has been reduced and is hardly noticeable. I recommend it for all youngsters, women under 200 pounds, and men over 50 (years, not pounds). Because of the low recoil, three-shot factor and the fact that no pumping is required, I think it is the best type of shotgun for a beginner of any age or weight.

If you are an experienced hunter with your own pumps or doubles, by all means stick with them. One secret of shotgun shooting is to own a gun that fits you well, that you have practiced with, and whose capabilities you know and have confidence in. These considerations are more important than what type of shotgun it is.

Another of Charley's Principles states that a gunner will blame a bad day in the field on

A brace of mourning dove taken with a pump shotgun.

everything but himself. He changes guns, swaps shot sizes, and cusses his mother-in-law.

A shotgun is a tool used to overcome the distance factor between you and the quarry you want to acquire. A $100 shotgun off a store rack has as much inherent capability of causing the demise of a dove as a $4,000 shotgun. The expensive one has the advantage of being tailored to the original owner and perhaps bored to a specific choke. It may be gussied up, but just like any other gun, it still has to be pointed correctly. It does not shoot any harder or farther! A shotgun is simply an enclosed launching pad with a barrel to start the shot in a given direction with a certain pattern.

This was brought home to me rather forcefully many years ago when I was hunting with Claiborne Darden near Greensboro, North Carolina. At that time I owned what was an expensive double for me, but I was having a miserable time connecting with a dove. Claiborne, an excellent wing shooter, was doing almost as badly. As we took a break to commiserate with each other, a farm lad about 13 years old walked out

When the doves are covering you up, it's hard to be calm about reloading. The more you rush, the longer it takes.

Many youngsters start dove hunting early, consistent with state laws on age. (Photo credit: Oklahoma Department of Wildlife Conservation)

to the crest of a nearby knoll carrying a single-shot gun held together with baling wire. It was hot, and he was wearing one of those Jungle Jim helmets.

While complaining to Claiborne about my shotgun, I saw five doves flying directly toward the lad. The youngster waited calmly until the birds were almost to him, then he quickly raised the gun, swung, and pulled the trigger. A dove collapsed. The lad took off his helmet and caught the bird in it without moving a step!

"Claiborne," I said, "this heat is getting to me. Would you turn around and watch that farm boy on the hill?"

As we both watched, another flock of doves streaked toward the kid. He calmly waited, raised his gun, shot, and pulled off his helmet in one continuous motion. He knew the bird was dead when he pulled the trigger, but he did have to move a couple of steps to catch it in his helmet.

The boy repeated his performance twice more. I said, "I think I'll give up dove shooting."

"No," Claiborne replied, "let's move down the field where that lad can't see us shoot." We did, way down!

The difference, of course, was that the youngster had been pointing and swinging his cheap shotgun correctly. I had not been doing the same with my expensive double.

Let's say you need to buy a shotgun for dove hunting and you follow our suggestion to start with a semiautomatic, gas-operated type. What features do you look for in the semiautomatic or any other type? Without comparing brands and costs here, as you will do in a sporting goods store, I would like to say that I think all of the popular manufacturers are making good shotguns and that any one will last the average hunter a lifetime if he takes proper care of it.

The first major consideration in buying a shotgun is fit. To learn about fit, go to a gun shop or a sporting goods dealer who specializes in firearms and ask for help. The great majority of hunters in America use shotguns of standard dimensions bought off the rack. Most are not perfect fits, but the hunters learn to shoot them by trial and error. There is good reason for this: custom-made shotguns, with dimensions tailored to one individual, are very expensive. (Also expensive are such extras as fancy walnut stocks, extra checkering, and gold engraving which will neither improve your shooting nor impress your quarry.)

If you purchase a standard gun, practice with it for a while on clay targets. Should you later decide that the fit is causing you to shoot inaccurately, take it to a gunsmith for modifications. Do not allow well-meaning hunting buddies to tamper with *your* gun.

Unless you are used to a rib on other shotgun barrels, the expense of a matted or ventilated rib is not necessary. A plain barrel is adequate. Because dove hunting generally does not involve much walking, the weight of a shotgun should

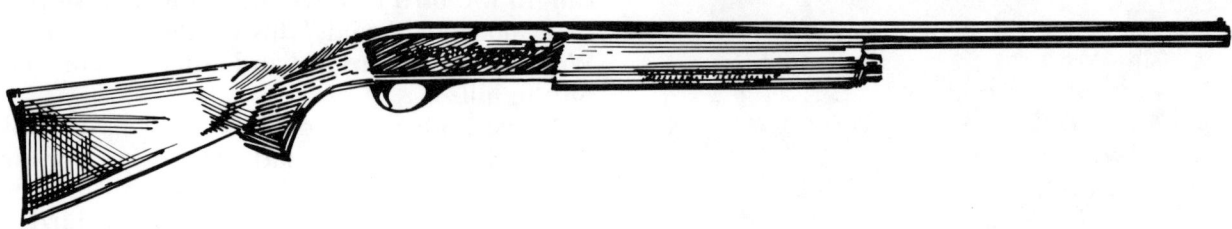

not figure critically in your selection. Many hunters, who have several guns for a variety of wing and clay-target shooting, try to buy them or adjust them to the same weight for smooth, consistent swinging. Light guns have more recoil than heavier guns, but this is a negligible factor in gas-operated semiautomatics.

Three factors you must decide on when purchasing any shotgun are gauge, choke, and barrel length. Much of the nomenclature for shotguns and shells has evolved haphazardly—it is not an attempt by manufacturers to confuse people. I'm sure they would gladly change some nomenclature except that the shooters who have already mastered the names would raise a howl.

Gauge indicates the size shell you use in a shotgun. Gauge is a measurement of the bore, or inside diameter of the barrel. Many years ago, a gun's bore size was measured by the number of round lead balls in a pound that fit the bore. For instance, the bore of a 12-gauge gun could be fitted by a round ball twelve of which weighed one pound. The designation is still used. The lower the gauge number, the larger the bore and the larger the shell used. A 12-gauge shotgun (or shell), accordingly, is larger than a 20-gauge.

Most shotguns in America come in one of six sizes; five are designated by gauge and one, the .410-inch bore shotgun, by inch. When the manufacturers are making shotguns, they don't run around melting lead balls to measure things—they use inches. For clarification of shotgun sizes, the following are average inch equivalents: 10-gauge, .775 inch; 12-gauge, .730 inch; 16-gauge, .670 inch; 20-gauge, .615 inch; 28-gauge, .550 inch; and 410 bore, .410 inch. So that you won't lie awake all night wondering, the .410 bore figures out to a 67½-gauge. I can hardly wait to see what happens when America switches to the metric system!

To make your selection easier, three sizes can be eliminated from the list—the 10, 28, and .410. The 10-gauge shotgun is a semiobsolete cannon used by a few waterfowlers; new shells with correct shot sizes for doves are no longer being manufactured for the 10-gauge, and a gun this large is not needed for dove hunting. The 28-gauge is mostly used for shooting skeet; shells are difficult to find in many areas and the gauge is too small except for expert field shooters. The .410 bore shotgun shoots too light a load to be considered by anyone except master shooters. It is unfair to the dove because it more often cripples than kills cleanly, and it is unfair to the beginner because he will not bag enough doves to gain confidence in his shooting. Yet thousands of fathers start their youngsters on .410s when the old man himself couldn't hit the broad side of a barn with one.

This leaves the 12-, 16-, and 20-gauge guns. The 16 would seem to be a happy medium, and I am generally a great one for compromise with equipment. If you have hunted or fished very much, you know there is no such thing as a perfect piece of equipment for all conditions you may encounter, and you accordingly select your gear for what you expect to happen *most* of the time.

However, for the following reasons I would bypass the 16. Some manufacturers of fine gas-

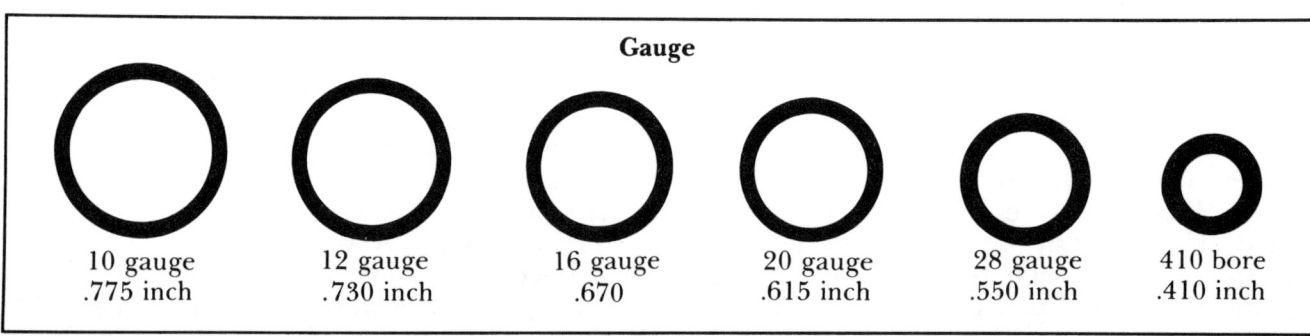

operated semiautomatics do not make them in 16-gauge. Some choices of 20-gauge shells equal or approach low-power 16-gauge loads. The 16-gauge shotgun has decreased in popularity, and its resale is not as easy as for the 12- or 20-gauge.

This narrows your selection to two gauges. With the wide choice of brands available, weight does not have to be a factor in making a selection. Some 12-gauges of one brand weigh no more than 20-gauges of another brand. The diameter of a 20-gauge shot pattern at effective killing range is the same diameter as a 12-gauge pattern fired through an identical choke. The big difference is that the 12-gauge has a denser pattern.

I recommend that the beginner start with a 12-gauge shotgun for mourning doves. It is better than the 20 for whitewings and should definitely be used on bandtails which are difficult birds to bring down cleanly. Nothing gives a new shooter confidence and peps him up like knocking down birds; all things being equal, he will knock more down with a 12-gauge.

Shotgun Shells

A 12-gauge can also be used for large game such as ducks, pheasants, and turkeys. (You may need to buy an interchangeable barrel with a different choke to cover different ranges.) The 12-gauge is also ideal for smaller game such as grouse and woodcock. For the beginning to average shooter, the 12-gauge is the all-around, all-purpose gauge.

It is a rare day when the beginner or average hunter "blows up" a bird on the wing because he was shooting a 12-gauge rather than a 20-gauge. He is not overgunned with a 12-gauge! Mourning doves are the most difficult winged game on the continent to shoot. The beginner needs the advantages of the larger 12-gauge shot load. The true sportsman goes afield properly gunned. There is nothing sporting about being undergunned and crippling doves.

Well, where does that leave the 20-gauge? Hopefully, in the hands of experienced shooters of proven ability where it belongs. For the experienced gunner who shoots only when doves are within the right range for his choke, the 20-gauge has a definite place.

Later on in the chapters on shooting, I hope to convince you that 95 percent of the hunters should not try to hit doves over 40 or 45 yards away. Much of the secret to successful dove shooting lies in letting the birds come inside this range before firing. By learning to judge range, using range aids, wearing camouflage, using blinds or cover and decoys, and in selecting a good shooting site, you increase your chances of getting within this 40- to 45-yard radius and hitting them.

The choke is the bore constriction of a shotgun barrel at the muzzle which concentrates the shot for its flight through the air. Different amounts of constriction give differently sized patterns of shot charge. The degree of choke is measured by the approximate percentage of pellets which hit within a 30-inch circle at 40 yards. The following table gives percentage with various chokes.

Full choke	65 to 75%	Full choke
Improved modified	55 to 65%	¾ choke
Modified	45 to 55%	½ choke
Improved cylinder	35 to 45%	¼ choke
Cylinder	25 to 35%	No choke

Most companies manufacture standard shotguns in three chokes—full, modified, or improved cylinder. Improved modified and cylinder chokes generally have been discontinued, but a gunsmith can ream out a full choke to improved modified or improved cylinder to cylinder. Very expensive custom guns can be ordered with a fairly specific choke, such as 40 percent for the right barrel and 75 percent for the left barrel.

The table above is the old system of measuring which is still in effect. However, in recent years manufacturers have so greatly improved shotshells that the patterns are tighter than the tables would indicate. For instance, your full choke shotgun might pattern a higher percentage at 40 yards than shown. To put it another way, the 65 to 75 percent shown for 40 yards might register that high at 45 yards or more.

As a shot charge leaves the muzzle, it begins to

spread into a cone shape. The farther it travels, the more it spreads and the longer the shot string becomes. If you look at the choke table, you'll see that shot fired from a barrel with cylinder choke (that is, no choke) spreads so rapidly that by the time it travels 40 yards only 25 to 35 percent of the shot would hit within a 30-inch circle. With the other extreme, full choke, the pattern would hold together so that 65 to 75 percent of the pellets would hit inside the circle.

If you wanted to hit a flying target at 10 yards, your choice of choke would be cylinder; the shot spreads quickly, and an open pattern increases your chances at this distance. On the other hand, if you shot at a dove at 45 yards with a cylinder choke, your shot would be so widely spread that the bird could fly through it without being touched.

At another extreme, let's say you tried to hit a dove at 10 yards with a *full-choked gun*. The pattern would be so tight it would almost be like shooting a bullet, and your chances of connecting would be very slim. However, at 40 yards the pattern would be opening just right, and your chances of hitting the bird would be increased.

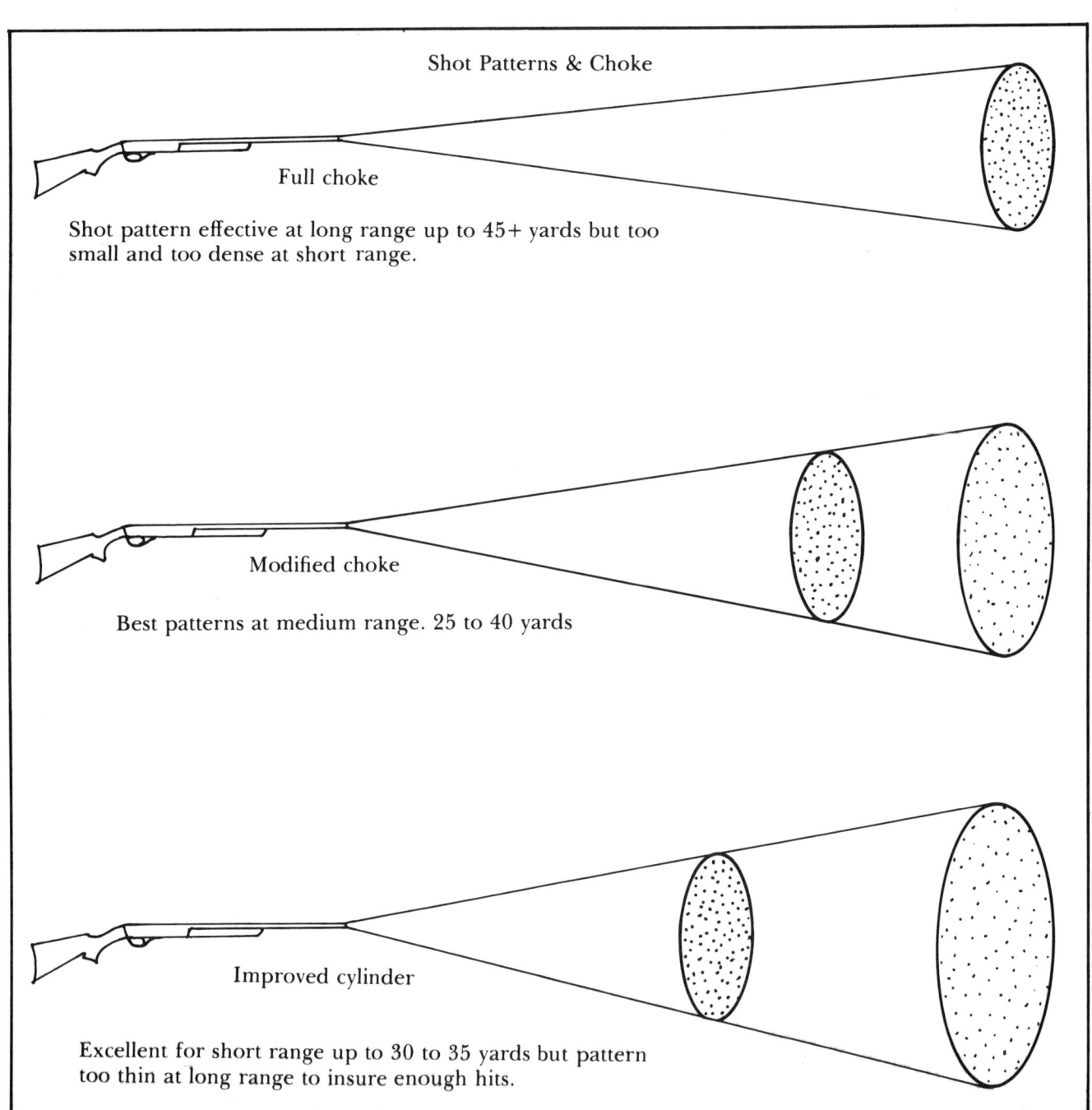

Shot Patterns & Choke

Full choke

Shot pattern effective at long range up to 45+ yards but too small and too dense at short range.

Modified choke

Best patterns at medium range. 25 to 40 yards

Improved cylinder

Excellent for short range up to 30 to 35 yards but pattern too thin at long range to insure enough hits.

When dove hunting, you may shoot at one bird at 15 yards and the next at 40 yards. Obviously you cannot have the perfect pattern of shot spread and density for both shots. Therefore, your decision on what choke to use is based on the average range at which you expect to take most shots. You have to compromise.

The Federal Cartridge Corporation offers the following guide to make choke selection easier. Improved cylinder choke is recommended for short range shooting from 30 to 35 yards; a modified choke has the best patterns at medium ranges, from 25 to 45 yards; the full choke has effective patterns at long range, from 50 to 55 yards, but the patterns are too small and too dense at short range.

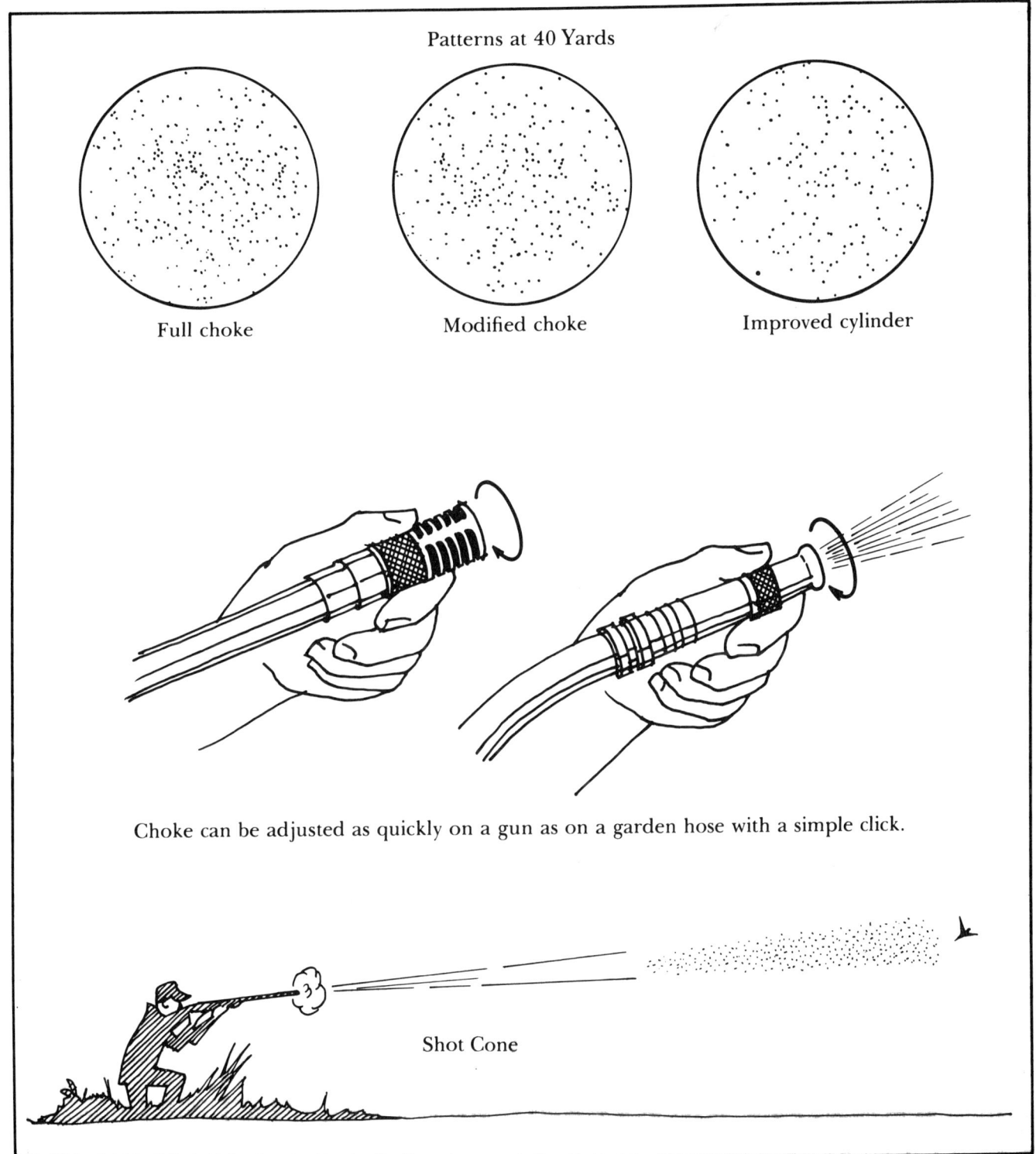

Patterns at 40 Yards

Full choke — Modified choke — Improved cylinder

Choke can be adjusted as quickly on a gun as on a garden hose with a simple click.

Shot Cone

There are not many field situations which call for a full choke. It may be needed when bandtails come in high over tall trees, for jump-shooting doves, and for spooked whitewings. However, the beginning and average hunters have enough trouble trying to hit doves at short and medium ranges without trying to hit them at 50 or 55 yards. In fact, there are very few hunters who can consistently kill doves cleanly at 50 and 60 yards. It isn't that all of us don't get plenty of chances. But most of us are not good enough with a shotgun to handle long ranges. If we try, the result is a low batting average and, much worse, we often injure birds that fly away and die two or three days later.

On opening day and during the early part of the dove and whitewing seasons, the birds whiz in close to the shooters. A full-choked gun has too tight a pattern at these short ranges. In fact, throughout the entire season you will find that many of the shots you missed were at close range. The dove that dives in on you and tries to take your cap off wraps you up in knots! It's easy to waste three shells on him.

For the above reasons, I would suggest that the new or average hunter forget about the full choke. All of the outstanding shooters I have seen around the nation (i.e., the ones with a low expenditure of shells per bird bagged) let the birds come within 45 to 35 yards, or closer, and pass up the long shots.

I recommend that the beginning or average hunter select a modified choke if he plans to shoot a semiautomatic or a pump. If he uses a double, the barrels should be choked improved cylinder and modified. These are satisfactory choices based on which choke is best *most* of the time.

Many hunters in the South use their quail guns for doves. The single barrels are usually improved cylinder. Some hunters use light loads but many prefer heavy loads to increase the pattern density. By shooting only at doves within 35 yards, some of these hunters are deadly. There is nothing wrong with letting a dove come in range! In fact, it's the sporting thing to do.

There are several adjustable choke devices which can be fitted on the muzzle so that you can change your choke while hunting to fit the range most of the birds are flying. One of the best is a Poly-Choke, which acts much like the nozzle on a hose. Simply turn the nozzle and you get different sprays, or choke.

The Poly-Choke has nine settings ranging from cylinder to extra-full. To get one installed, you or your dealer must ship your barrel to the factory. For detailed information, write: Poly-Choke, Box 296, Hartford, Connecticut 06101.

Most shotgun barrels are manufactured in 26-, 28-, and 30-inch lengths. The 30-inch barrel does not shoot any harder or farther than the 26-inch barrel. Longer barrels are preferred by some shooters because of the longer sight radius and more accurate pointing. Other hunters prefer shorter barrels because of the faster handling.

It's really a matter of personal preference. If you're an experienced hunter, you know what you like. If you're fairly new to hunting, start with the 28-inch barrel. Poly-Choke recommends an overall length of 27 inches with its device installed, although they'll install for any overall length you want.

When you buy a new shotgun, you will want to pattern it. The easiest way to do this is to buy part or all of a roll of inexpensive wrapping paper at least 40 inches wide. Cut off about six feet of the strong section of a heavy cane fishing pole. Go to a safe place in the woods, insert the pole through the roll and wire the pole between two scrub trees as high as you can reach.

Pull a length of the paper to the ground, and place a couple of rocks on a folded edge to keep the paper spread. Pace off 40 yards, and you are ready to pattern your gun. Shoot at the center of the taut paper; then leave your gun and shells at the shooting spot and walk to the paper. Cut off the section with holes and flatten it on the ground.

Standard Poly-Choke

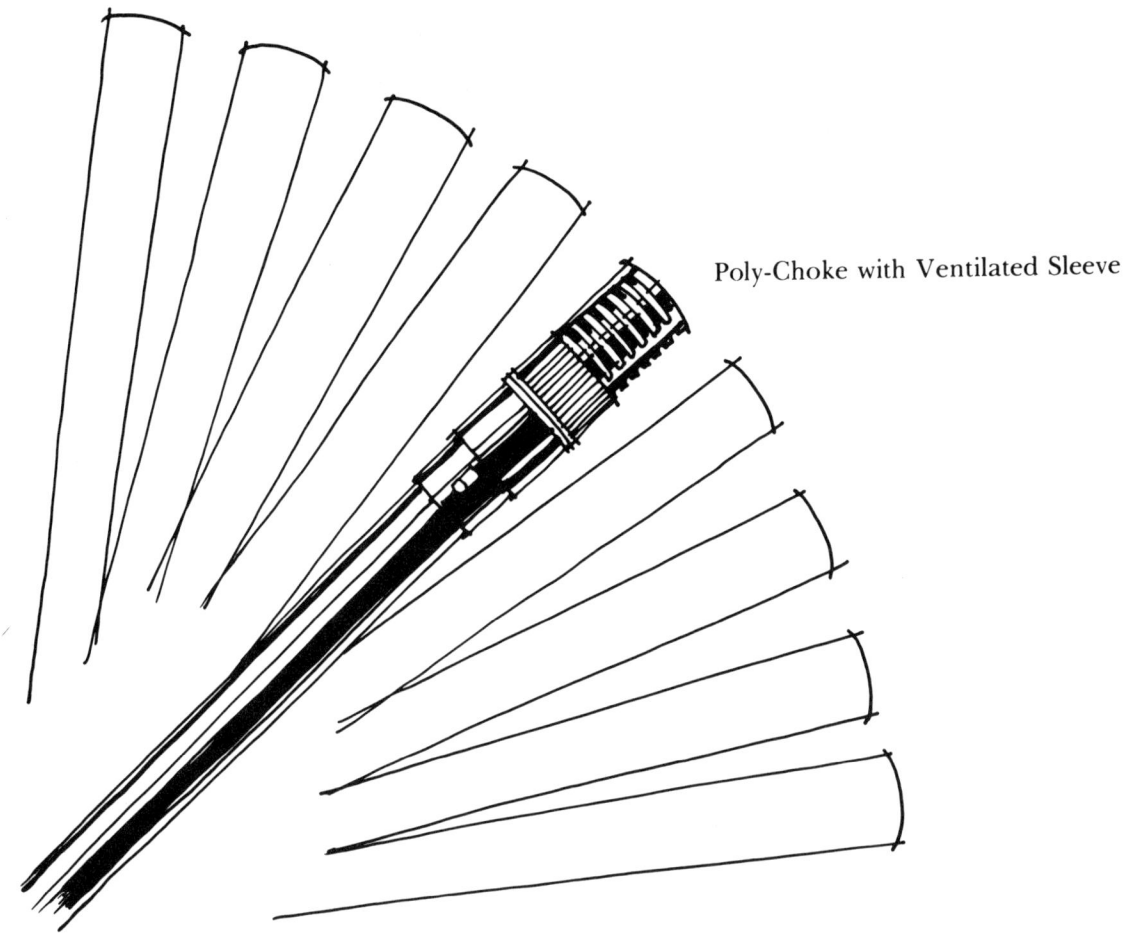

Poly-Choke with Ventilated Sleeve

Take a soft lead pencil with a 15-inch string attached to it. Pick a spot in the center of where the shot is concentrated; hold the tip of the string there and make a circle with the pencil. You now have a 30-inch circle to measure the percentage of shot from the load you fired.

Count the shot holes inside the circle. From the table of lead shot pellets per ounce, figure the number of pellets you fired. Let's say you fired one ounce of number 8 shot; that would mean about 410 pellets. Let's say you count 205 holes in the paper. Divide 410 pellets into 205, and you get 50 percent. This means your barrel has a modified choke.

At this stage, you may well ask if it wouldn't be easier to read the choke stamped on the barrel than to go to all this trouble. It would, and, of course, you knew what choke it was before you bought the gun. However, there are a number of good reasons for testing your own gun.

Every barrel is not tested before it leaves the factory. Some companies only test by lot, that is, one out of a batch. A given barrel does not necessarily pattern different-sized pellets alike: one may have a superior density which would influence your choice of shot size for birds.

You will want to put a small strip of bright tape in the center of the paper and deliberately aim and fire it. Several shots show the accuracy of your gun. I once bought a new barrel which fired five feet off at 40 yards. It was a built-in excuse for missing, but I sent it back to the factory and had it fixed anyway.

Another reason for test-firing is to help you understand shot pattern.

To test a particular shotshell load, you should fire several times at the paper and take an average. By trying different loads and shot sizes, you may find one that is far better than the others.

After this first testing, you will have a good understanding of your pattern at 40 yards. But all of your field shots will not be at 40 yards. Fire several times from distances of 35, 30, 25, 20, and 15 yards. It will help you to understand how your pattern spreads and the capability of your gun.

One word of caution in making your evalua-

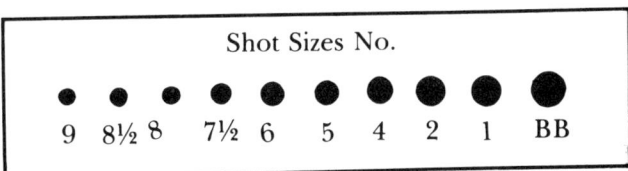

tion: when you look at the holes in the paper, you are seeing a two-dimensional result of a three-dimensional shot cone. The farther a shot string travels, the more it strings lengthwise. All pellets which hit your paper did not do so at the same time, although it "looks" that way.

When you are shooting a moving target, you have a chance of hitting it with more pellets if the shot string is short. A dove on the wing does not wait for lagging shot to catch up. When patterning a gun on paper, remember that the third-dimensional factor of shot string does not show.

A dove is about 12 inches square from his head to the tip of his tail and from wing tip to wing tip. One shot pellet can bring a dove down if it cracks the skull, breaks the neck, or splinters a wing bone. That is a matter of chance, not accuracy. The other vital area, the one we shoot at, is the body. It's about like shooting at a billiard ball. On the average, I believe, it takes at least three to five pellets in the body to bring a dove down cleanly. This means hitting the bird with a concentrated part of your pattern with shot of the right weight and velocity.

Other than chance shots, most doves are knocked down by shock. The impact of a certain number of shot produces shock from weight and velocity; shock is increased by penetration. Because of the thickness of the breast of the dove, shot seldom penetrates to such vital organs in the body cavity as the heart or lungs.

Shot begins to lose speed shortly after leaving the muzzle. Tests on one 12-gauge load with number 6 shot showed a muzzle velocity of 1,400 feet a second; at 40 yards the shot had slowed to 800 feet per second and at 60 yards to 665 feet per second. This shows why it is difficult to kill birds cleanly at long ranges. With the rapid drop of speed, it is hard to lead the bird correctly, and if the bird is hit, the shock factor has decreased. Small shot lose speed faster than large shot.

Whatever the gauge of your shotgun, there are several things to consider in selecting a box of shells. Brand is not critical except where price may be concerned. All of the manufacturers are making shells superior to anything on the market a few years ago. Besides, over 90 percent of the shells in the United States are produced by just three companies, regardless of the number of brand names you see. When you have a good day afield with one brand, that's the one you'll decide is best. It *does* help to have faith in the brand you shoot; it's mostly mental, but it helps.

Your shotgun is chambered to take a shell of a certain length—for our purposes, 2¾ inches—before it is loaded. We will not consider three-inch shells made for shotguns with chambers of three inches. This is more gun and ammo than is needed or practical. Shell length before loading is printed on every box. There are 25 shells to a box.

The powder in a shell is designated on the box in one of two ways. For some heavy loads, it says "Max" for maximum, rather than a specific weight. With most shells, the powder is listed by black "powder equivalent drams," although all

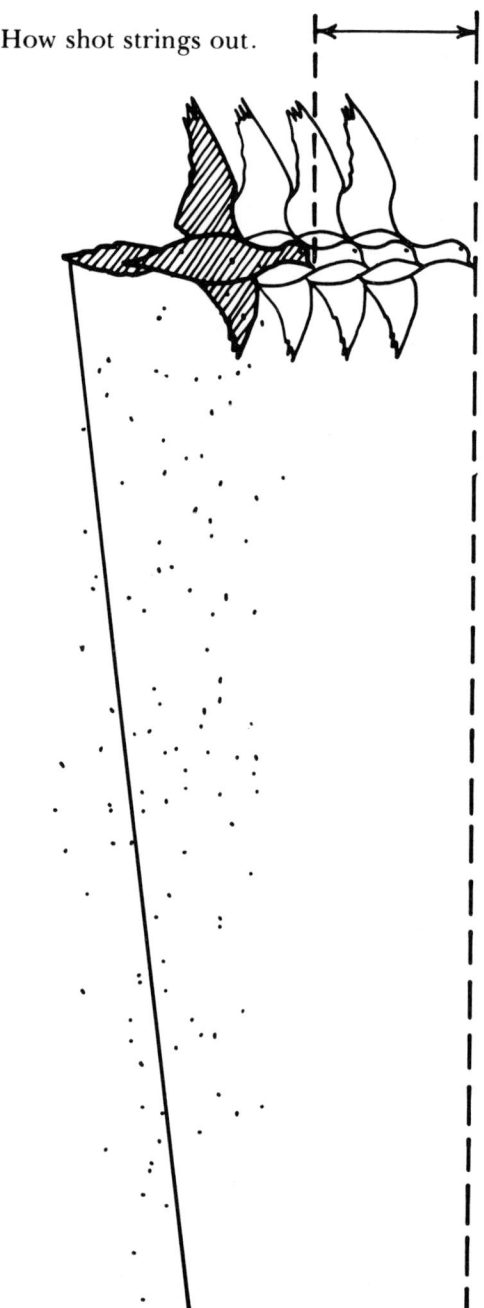

How shot strings out.

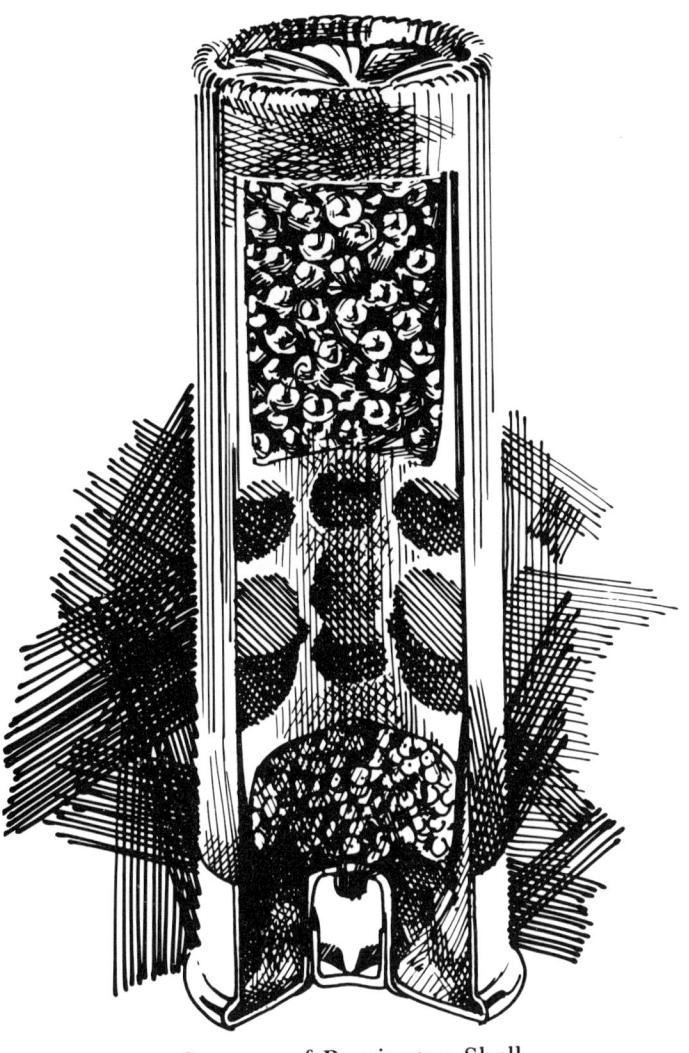

Cutaway of Remington Shell

factory shells are loaded with modern smokeless powder. There are 16 drams to an ounce. If the box says "3¼ powder equivalent drams," that means your shell's smokeless powder is the equivalent of 3¼ drams of black powder.

The shell box lists by ounce the weight of shot in each shell. No matter what brand of shell you buy and how the loads vary, the powder and shot weights are balanced for a particular performance.

Shot pellets are measured by diameter in fractions of an inch. They are designated by number. The higher the number, the smaller the shot. That is, #9 is smaller in diameter than #8 or #6.

Any box of shells you buy will be clearly marked with the manufacturer's name, code number, gauge, shell length, powder, weight of shot, and size of shot. If you are a new shooter and, quite understandably, are confused by all this nomenclature, ask the sporting goods dealer to help you select the right shells.

For our purposes there are four general types of 2¾-inch shells by load with some overlapping. The Magnum is the most powerful but is really needed only for long-range bandtail or whitewing shooting. The second most powerful shell is the high-power or high-brass, with each company using its own designation such as Express, Super, or Hi-Power. The third most powerful is the field load. The lightest are target shells, mostly sold and used at gun clubs for skeet and trap. Target shells are the only ones currently loaded with #8½ shot.

You need only to choose between the high-power and the field load for mourning doves. Any shell in either category will do if you shoot within the recommended ranges of your choke. The high-power is a stronger load, but I'd like for you to think of the high-power shells as providing a more dense shot pattern rather than giving extra distance. You will recall that shot pattern at 40 yards is measured by percentage. A heavier shot load will mean more pellets in the 30-inch circle.

If we eliminate the #8½ target shot, four sizes are left to choose from—#9, #8, #7½, and #6. Larger shot are not to be considered; you don't use a turkey load to kill a dove. Except for the first few days of the mourning dove season when birds are not wary and may fly in close, I suggest you forget about #9 shot. It is too small.

Hunters love to argue about whether it is more effective to use lots of smaller shot or fewer larger pellets. They will still be discussing it on Judgement Day. I prefer the extra shock of the larger pellets. My rule of thumb on selecting shot size is, when there's a choice, lean toward the larger pellets.

For nearly all dove hunting, I recommend #7½ or #8 shot. Either is excellent if the gun is pointed in the right direction and you do not take wild shots at birds out of range for your choke. If you expected whitewings to be mixed with the mourning doves, you'd certainly choose the larger #7½. For whitewings and bandtails use #7½ or #6.

The field loads are designed to do the job. If you want to soup up your load by using high-power shot, do it for pattern density and shocking power rather than for long shots.

This chapter has been a lengthy discussion in order to give you some of the basic information for making decisions. Don't let all the nomenclature and options throw you! What's important is to choose one shotgun and one happy-medium load and stick with them.

Other Equipment

The following equipment is optional, but some of it may help with your shooting and make you more comfortable afield.

Charley's Law states that a dove hunter should "travel light"—that is, be able to carry easily all his gear with him at one time when on the move.

I have been on a few fancy dove hunts where a guest was not allowed to tote so much as his own shotgun and probably walked no more than 25 yards all afternoon. Each guest was assigned a "pickup" boy who also doubled as gun bearer. We were driven to the blinds and comfortably seated in them. The pickup boy watched for approaching doves and let you know when it looked as though they were coming in.

Whenever I knocked a bird down, the pickup boy would run out and retrieve it. About every half hour, a truck loaded with huge ice chests of soft drinks and snacks would stop by the blinds and minister to our needs. When a limit was reached, the truck would haul us to the farmhouse. The pickup boy would oil my gun, disappear for a few minutes, and return with my dressed doves. My greatest exertion all afternoon was to shove shells into my gun and raise it to shoot.

I have never refused an invitation to a fancy shoot, but it is not my favorite way of hunting. I don't feel comfortable having someone else carry my gun, spot my birds, and pick them up. I really enjoy toting my gun and other equipment and handling things on my own, as do most hunters.

Another of Charley's Laws says that outdoorsmen new at hunting or fishing have a tendency to take more gear than they need or use. The more experienced they get, the less they tote.

Let's review your hunting equipment. For any shoot lasting over an hour, I recommend some kind of stool. As strange as it seems, it is difficult to find a place in the field to sit comfortably. If you sit on the ground, you are a magnet for ants and other creepy-crawlers. If a dove sneaks in, there's an awkward scramble to rise, get your gun mounted and rush off one departing shot.

A city hunter may be able to walk steadily for two or three hours but he has trouble standing for 30 minutes. He has to have something to lean against or sit on. He cannot kneel for long or his legs will go to sleep. I once left the field with a badly sprained ankle as a result of kneeling too long. When I jumped up to fire at a sneaky dove, my left leg was numb, and I collapsed in a heap.

A city hunter cannot squat to rest. His legs won't last more than five minutes. It takes a piney woods Cracker, a Tennessee ridge runner, or a Navajo Indian to rest in this position. I envy the rural squatter for I have seen him rest this way for hours at a time. It is a mysterious art I gave up trying to learn a long time ago.

It is easy to tote one of the many shooting stools now on the market. I use one which folds, has a shell and game bag with a zipper opener, under the canvas seat, and a small shoulder strap. The frame is made of aluminum, and the stool parts are colored green and khaki, ideal camouflage colors. These stools will last a long time if you do not walk off and leave them in the field. Mine cost $10.00 five years ago, and I expect it to last several more years.

The shooting stool improves my shooting by letting me rest comfortably between dove flights and be relaxed with no strained or tired muscles when the birds come in. As I rise from a sitting or standing position, I mount the gun, losing no more time in this quick movement than if I were standing.

It is easy to make a light seat. Some hunters take a wooden crate, cover half of the opening with wood for inside storage of shells and birds,

All of the equipment you need to bag doves—three styles of shooting stools, decoys, a small cooler, machete, shotguns, camouflage clothing, shells, and a ham setter who wants to look into the camera.

and paint it green or brown. Small oil drums are also convertible. A cushion can be made for the top and a section of metal cut out to allow entrance for storage.

Shot doves should be allowed to cool as much as field conditions will allow. About all you can do is space them in the shade. It's best not to confine them in a game bag or shooting stool until you decide to change locations or leave the field. The temperature of a live mourning dove is usually between 104° and 105°. In some September shooting, a shot dove doesn't cool much before it's the same temperature as the air. If you keep the birds out of metal containers on hot days, there's nothing to worry about. Dove shoots seldom last more than two or three hours, and your birds will be out of the field before there is time for them to spoil.

Of all the kinds of hunting in America, the only one which comes close to having a uniform is dove hunting. Most dove hunters wear some combination of camouflage garments. There are two reasons. They have found that doves fly in closer and that camouflage clothing is inexpensive.

Hunter movement is what the dove picks up with its eyes. Movement spooks doves. Camouflage clothing helps to conceal movement.

Any experienced hunter can recall being caught in an open field by an incomer. He remained completely still, not craning his neck or moving his face, and the dove continued to fly toward him. Not until the dove got within range did he raise his gun into position; when the dove saw this movement he, of course, veered, but by this time it was too late (for the bird).

Apparently, doves have difficulty in recognizing a motionless human as an enemy. Perhaps this depends on how much hunting pressure the birds have been exposed to. Anyway, it's a fact

Camouflage clothing helps hide movement from approaching doves, and wearing it means you'll get more shooting.

that most hunters move around too much when doves are approaching. They stand up and wave their guns when the birds are 100 yards away. They are unable to wait until the doves are in range before making their move to shoot. Camouflage clothing helps cover these blunders: by breaking up the hunter's silhouette and masking movement it enables the hunter to blend in with his surroundings.

Camouflage suits of coats and britches sell for as little as $10.00 or $12.00. GI surplus stores usually have a variety of designs, though most of the clothes are straight from a factory and not surplus.

In selecting a suit, take several factors into consideration. First, since much dove shooting is done during hot weather, and since it is harder to stay cool in hot weather than it is warm in cold weather, cotton is generally the best fabric for year-round comfort. It breathes. Even if it gets soaked with perspiration, there is a cooling effect from evaporation.

Nylon can be very hot, and it snags easily on briars, and rips.

Your camouflage suit should be a little large so that your shoulders and arms are not bound when you mount and swing your gun. Also, consider that for cool weather you may wish to wear a shirt and sweater under your jacket.

The pockets should be deep for carrying shells, and each should have a button or zipper. You will find some brands whose pockets are so shallow that you could not possibly pick up a bird or crawl through a fence without spilling shells. I usually carry two or three boxes of shells to the field in my shooting stool, put 10 or 15 shells in my pocket for quick loading, and refill from the boxes as necessary. To avoid littering, I pick up the spent hulls after the shoot and carry them out in the shooting stool. Reloaders are always glad to get the extra hulls.

Try to find a camouflage suit with pockets in the pants too, as you will need the space for your wallet, hunting license, knife, and other articles.

Some hunters wear a camouflage jacket and green or khaki britches, figuring they'll be standing in cover for most of the shooting. In extremely hot weather, some hunters wear a drab or camouflaged shooting vest with nothing under it. If you hunt very much, you'll see every kind of variation. Your guiding principle should be that the better you camouflage yourself, the more shooting you'll get.

Wear a camouflage cap or hat. You may need the bill to shade out sun and, more importantly, to mask your continual head movement. The bill helps to hide your face which most often gives you away to a dove.

Hunters are quite conservative in their buying habits: if camouflage were not effective, you wouldn't see so many hunters in recent years changing to it.

At this point, you may be wondering if the hunter shouldn't cover his face and gun with camouflage grease paint and remove his wrist watch so that it does not flash. I do this for a lot of crow shooting but have not found it necessary for doves. Should grease paint ever become essential for successful shooting, however, I'll gladly dab it on.

One final reason for wearing camouflage—if the doves are acting scared and cautious, you don't want to be the only one of 10 or 20 hunters who *isn't* wearing camouflage. They'll all blame you for spooking the birds.

There is little walking in most types of dove shooting; nevertheless, your shoes or boots should be selected for comfort. If you hunt where there may be poisonous snakes, you'll undoubtedly be more at ease if you wear thick or snakeproof boots.

Many trap and skeet shooters wear shatterproof glasses when they hunt. They have learned to protect their eyes on clay target fields. Also, lenses of certain colors such as amber make a target or bird stand out more clearly. Shades of grays and greens are restful to the eyes on bright days.

Shatterproof lenses protect your eyes from stray pellets and also protect your eyes when you shoot in the general direction of the sun. If you are swinging your gun to catch up with a dove, it is very easy to look directly at the sun, and without sunglasses, you'll be blinded for a few seconds. If you do this often enough, you can damage your eyes permanently. In the course of a shoot, it's surprising how many doves will come into or leave a field with the sun as a background.

During the dove season, I usually leave a

machete in my car trunk. Although it's not needed on many hunts, it does come in handy for clearing a spot in heavy cover to shoot from. If I have to build a quick blind in an open field, the machete is perfect for cutting branches and weeds. The long blade is also used for sharpening branches and weed stalks so that they can easily be stuck into the ground. My machete is also used as a hammer for driving small stakes into the ground as range markers.

Many shooters use surplus GI metal ammo boxes for storing shells and freshly shot doves which is a fine idea as long as neither becomes overheated. Shells can be damaged from long exposure to excessive heat and, of course, you don't want to simmer your doves.

A four-wheel-drive vehicle or other field car is seldom needed for dove hunting, unless you are planning to climb logging roads in the mountains to reach bandtail country. The family car, the trunk of which provides valuable storage space for gear, is quite suitable for most dove hunting. Parking the car 100 yards or so from the shooting field will help keep the birds from spooking.

It's a good idea to keep an ice chest in the car, rather than taking it to the blinds; it can be used to keep food cool and to ice down whole or dressed birds.

For those first days of the season when the mercury is hovering around 95° and the humidity is at wet-blanket level, you can get very uncomfortable if the birds are not flying (if your field is being smothered by doves, you won't care if you're in the middle of a heat wave or a snowstorm). A canteen in the stands can provide welcome refreshment, preferably filled with God's greatest thirst quencher—water. On excessively hot days, I follow the advice of General Erwin Rommel to his Afrika Corps. I hold off

A machete is not required equipment, but it comes in handy for building a blind quickly.

taking the first drink of water as long as I can. Once I start, a barrel is not enough.

I always carry a first aid kit and insect repellant in the trunk of my car—in a large hunting party, someone will always need a headache remedy or some adhesive tape. As for insects, there's usually something that wants to feed on you, whether it is mosquitos, chiggers, or gnats. It's hard to concentrate on your shooting when you're being bitten.

Not many dove hunters use decoys for the simple reason that they don't go hunting until they've located a concentration, and then the decoys are not needed. Under certain situations decoys work. The dove is great for fellowship and doesn't have to have a formal introduction to join up with any stragglers he sees.

There are several brands of decoys on the market—you can buy them at a sporting goods store or order from mail-order houses. The decoy I use has a clothespin on the bottom which makes it easy to snap onto a branch or fence wire. It's also handy for putting on bare ground near a water hole by kicking out an area of dirt about the size of the pin.

The major problem with decoys under most conditions is getting them high enough in a bare tree so that they can be easily seen by doves. I don't want to use decoys badly enough to take a stepladder to the field; also, it's very time consuming to shinny up a tree to put out the decoys and later have to go back up the tree to get them down.

Most hunters compromise by attaching decoys to bare bushes or small trees. Sometimes you can bend a limb down enough to attach the decoy and then ease it back to its original height of 10 feet or so.

I have never been successful with decoys pulling large flocks of doves. A flight 50 yards high, obviously uninterested in your field, will not peel off simply because they spot your decoys. Generally, the doves which decoy are singles or in twos or threes, either confused by the shooting or simply looking for company. I suspect that young birds decoy more readily than older birds.

Since doves change flight direction so often even when there is no shooting, it is difficult to tell whether a dove flies your way because he spotted your decoys or because of some vague reason known only to the dove. I think that doves sometimes get so addled that they want to sit down and look around. Under this condition, if a bird sees your decoys he may well land among them.

Decoys, to be effective on the ground or in trees, must be placed so the doves can see clear silhouettes. Other than pulling a dove within your shooting range, decoys have another advantage. Approaching birds, whose eyes are focused on the decoys, are not as likely to see any movements you make.

When I use decoys, I usually carry about eight or ten with their clothespins attached to a rope draped across my shoulders. With my other equipment, that's as many as I can handle, though I think that the more you put up the better results you will have.

Decoys are optional for most dove hunting but fun to experiment with. They may pay off by attracting birds to your area when there are not enough hunters to cover a large field or pond. For the lone hunter who loves to try new techniques, there is a certain fascination in arranging decoys and pulling doves that he might otherwise not have had a shot at.

There are a number of dove calls on the market with which it is easy to imitate the calling of courting and mated doves. The mouth call will get a reply from doves, but it will not pull them in to the gun during the shooting season. It is of no value for hunting, but it is fun for the dove student who wishes to talk to birds during the mating season. After a poor day of shooting, I'm sometimes talking *at* the birds past midnight.

Dogs

Teaming up with a well-trained hunting dog is a pleasure for any type of wing shooting. Having a retrieving dog in a dove field will improve your shooting—you won't get sidetracked worrying about finding dead or crippled birds, and you can concentrate on handling your shotgun.

One of Charley's Laws states that no matter where a shot dove falls, it will be hard to find—you can drop one on a billiard table and still lose it.

A dead dove camouflages into anything it falls into—soil, leaves, weeds, corn shucks, or grass. It melts into a bare field and is even hard to see on a sand dune. A dog trained to retrieve can track by smell in dense cover what the human eye might not ever discover.

Taking a dog along on dove hunts is also one of the best conservation steps a hunter can practice. The annual crippling loss is 26 to 29 percent of the current harvest of about 50 million mourning doves, according to the Fish and Wildlife Service. In other words, for every 50 million doves bagged, about 13.7 million are lost.

If every hunting party used retrieving dogs, some crippled doves would still get away; doves are very hardy birds and may carry shot a mile or two before dropping. However, a good Labrador retriever will find nearly every bird that falls within a quarter of a mile of his handler. If more retrieving dogs were used, probably millions of crippled doves would be recovered.

A true sportsman makes every effort to find a dead or crippled bird. Aside from the humanitarian desire to dispatch an injured bird, it is a good conservation measure and wise use of a natural resource to recover as high a percentage of fallen birds as possible.

If you hunt without dogs you are apt to lose a downed bird no matter how well you mark it if you do not recover it immediately. The nature of dove shooting is such that the instant you start after a bird, you get another shot. Then you are surrounded by birds and get several more shots. You have three birds down, none well marked because of the shooting frenzy, and there's a good chance that you won't find all of them if there is much groundcover!

I know this to be true because it has happened to me many times. I have since learned to try to pick up each dove as quickly as it is downed, or right after a series of shots. Why drop two or three additional birds when it will be difficult enough to find those already down? Then, too, I can't shoot well when I am worried about losing crippled or dead birds. My conscience interferes. A good retrieving dog solves this problem, because you know he will mark and find fallen birds.

Unfortunately, there are a few hunters who deliberately do not pick up all their birds so that they can shoot more and still leave the field with only a limit. To prevent this wanton waste of migratory game birds, the federal regulations state: "No person shall kill or cripple any migratory game bird pursuant to this part without making a reasonable effort to retrieve the bird and include it in his daily bag limit."

The good sportsman need not worry about this provision, for he will search long and hard for each bird he downs. Also, I am anxious to find each bird for I may well have shot $3.00 worth of shells to down it.

Few hunters train dogs for dove shooting only. They usually take to the dove field a dog that has been trained on other game. For instance, retrievers such as Labradors and goldens are bred and trained to mark and fetch waterfowl and pheasants. Domestic pigeons are often used in training retrieving, springing, and pointing breeds, and this is all to the good.

English setter retrieves mourning dove from heavy cover for a happy hunter.

It's good conservation to hunt with a dog that will retrieve.

Field trials are not conducted for dogs to retrieve doves and wild pigeons, and there are no standards. It does not matter what breed is used for dove shooting as long as the dog will handle, has learned to mark birds, can smell well enough to locate doves, will retrieve them, and wants to perform these functions. One of the best working dogs I ever saw in a dove field was a German shepherd trained by a Texas rancher. I've also seen collies and mongrels that were efficient collectors. While I would prefer to see a hunting breed work, I do not care about the ancestry of the dog if he will locate doves and fetch them. Any working dog is a tool of conservation and better than no dog.

The retrieving breeds, such as Labradors and goldens, are generally best for dove shooting. They work equally well in water or on land. They'll pick up anything that falls, even if it doesn't have feathers on it. Goldens and Labs are friendly, amenable to handling, and have keen noses. Retrieving is bred into them!

Speaking of breed (not individual dogs), the Labrador retriever is the number one dog for dove shooting. A Lab will go through a dove field like a vacuum cleaner sucking up birds. He will fetch a bird which drops a mile away if he sees it go down. In fact, sometimes the Lab knows the bird was hit when the shooter thought he missed. The Lab will go after it and may be gone a long time, but when he returns he'll have a dove in his mouth.

I've seen a Lab handler work 30 blinds at a shoot and hardly miss a bird. During the shooting, the team would go from hunter to hunter asking if he had lost any birds. All the team needed was a direction. When the shooting stopped, the handler would make a final round for the Lab to pick up any unrecovered birds.

Some owners don't shoot as they get more fun out of working their dogs, and a lot more compliments. If there is just one dog retrieving at a shoot, many birds will be saved.

The springing breeds—springer and cocker spaniels—are excellent for either land or water retrieving. They are friendly dogs that perform with great spirit. Their long coats pick up all sorts of spurs and stickems which have to be combed out, but otherwise they are a pleasure to have along.

Pointing breeds that have been trained to retrieve quail, pheasant, or other game are adaptable to dove shooting. Pointers, setters, German shorthairs, Brittany spaniels, and others all can be trained for dove work both in water and on land. Naturally, the owner of a pointer used in field trials or highly trained for specialized work will not want to use him as a utility dog. However, the hunter who does a variety of hunting but can only own one or two dogs may well want to use his setter or Brit for retrieving doves.

A utility dog should be force-broken early, that is, taught to retrieve anything his master shoots, throws, or commands him to fetch. Sometimes force must be used to get across this message, but once this is accomplished, the dog is force-broken for life. The dog is taught to "hunt dead," to scent out a bird even if he did not see it fall, and to take his master's word that the bird is in the vicinity.

Apparently, doves and bandtails have a peculiar odor to dogs—one that is not appealing. Or perhaps they smell different from ground birds such as quail, grouse, and ringnecks. At any rate, pointing dogs which are good retrievers on other game often balk at picking up doves. Even some retrieving and springing dogs are reluctant to take doves into their mouths. The problem is compounded because dove feathers pull out easily, especially from young birds in hot weather. After a mouthful of dry feathers, a dog may understandably pussyfoot around before picking up another dove.

A dog force-broken to retrieve will usually pick up the first doves he finds—one advantage of taking the extra trouble to train him that way. He's well on his way to becoming a good dove dog on his first hunt.

The fact that a dog does not like the smell of

English setter fetches a dove for Jack Wingate, Bainbridge, Georgia.

doves or the taste of dry feathers is no excuse for not retrieving. I do not like paying his board all spring and summer when he is loafing, but I am obliged to do it. If we are to remain on friendly footing, my dog must fetch what I shoot. For the first few times I take a dog to a dove field, I carry a leash and choke collar, which the dog is well acquainted with from earlier training. If he balks, I put the choke collar on him and persuade him that it's in his best interest to perform as he's been taught with a training pad or other game.

Feathers do become a problem for the dog when there is a lot of retrieving on hot days, and a container of water is handy for washing feathers out of his mouth. In desert hunting, you may also need to wash the dog's nose when it gets clogged with dust. Also, if there are no ponds or wet drainage, drinking water must be carried to the field for the dog.

A young dog used for fetching doves should be broken in at shoots where there are no more than two or three hunters. This applies to dogs that have been used for other types of work where there were only two or three hunters. No matter how eager a dog is to retrieve, it is confusing to him to be put down in a field where there are maybe 20 or 30 hunters blasting away. He should be led gradually from smaller to larger hunts.

A dog taken to a shoot should be well under control. He should obey the basic commands of

Camouflaged hunter and his Lab on the alert for incoming doves.

This happy team is well hidden from view by their blind of dog fennel.

A handsome Labrador retiever gets first pull at a refreshing drink of water during a lull in the shooting.

fetch, whoa, sit, heel, and come. He will hear more shooting and see more birds than he has been accustomed to in other types of hunting, and it is only natural that he might get excited and tear around. You must be able to restrain him.

I am unconvinced that a dog running around in a field will spook doves. However, the hunters I'm shooting with may think so, and if birds are spooking while my dog is aimlessly running around, the other hunters will blame me. It's up to me to avoid this situation by keeping my dog at my station and making sure he goes straight to a fallen bird and comes directly back with it. I can't afford to lose invitations to future hunts.

Yellow or black Labs and golden retrievers usually blend in with the cover at a shooting stand. A dog with a lot of white, moving near the stand, undoubtedly attracts the attention of approaching doves. Although they are not afraid of the dog, the fact that they look my way may cause them to see me unless I'm camouflaged and hidden. A dog should be trained to sit where commanded—in shadows or low cover. The dog must be able to see the shooting to mark birds but at the same time be partially hidden or present a low profile.

If a dog is anxious to work and obeys basic commands, he quickly takes up the game and learns on his own to spot approaching birds. Sometimes he may see them before you do and let you know with a whine, or you glance at his alert head and know birds are coming in. He also learns to mark fallen birds or to dash out when you shoot and be almost under the bird when it falls, depending on how you have trained him. Most hunters let the dogs go on their own when they shoot. Dog specialists, usually retriever or springer people, make the dog sit until given a command to fetch. With whistle and hand signals, they can move their dogs around at 300 or 400 yards like border collies. It's not necessary for most hunting, but it's a real show of training, class, and style.

If you have your own dog you will get more shooting. You have to go where the doves are, not where you want them to be. In moving around to get under a flight line, you may have to pass up shooting opportunities if you don't have a dog, because shot birds may fall into cover where they are almost impossible to find. With a dog to find your birds, however, you are free to shoot.

For a small number of hunters shooting in a large field, a dog sometimes comes in handy for flushing doves that land to feed well out of spooking range. The dog is sent toward the doves, and after he gets them circling, he returns to his master. If the birds land in another distant spot, the dog is sent to put them up again.

The most dramatic illustration I have ever seen of the need for a retrieving dog was high in the Tehachapi Mountains of California. I was hunting bandtails with Carl Mills of Bakersfield; they were feeding on acorns on sharp ridges which jutted out from the rugged mountain range. We edged out on a spur, using the huge oak trees for cover, and got under the waves of bandtails which were just under a fog cap. I kept my utility setter, Smokey, at heel.

The first bandtail that Carl clobbered fell not more than 20 feet from us. The trouble was that it didn't stop. It hit a 70-degree slope, bounced, plunged, and rolled for at least 200 yards straight down. Smokey was after it in a flash, the first bandtail he'd ever seen. He slipped and skidded to the bird, grabbed it, and looked straight at us. It took him five minutes to wind his way back up over the talus and shaly cliff.

Of the 16 birds Carl and I shot that morning, only one landed where we could reach it. For the other 15, Smokey had to turn into a mountain goat. Without a dog along, we would not have been able to shoot because it would have been impossible for us to retrieve birds down those slopes and work back to the crest again. Smokey was awarded two steak bones that evening and given three nights off to chase stray bitches.

Although there are no statistics available, I believe more hunters than ever before are going afield with dogs which retrieve. It means more enjoyable hunting and is a great conservation measure.

Selecting a Shooting Site

When building a blind or choosing a stand or spot, take several factors into consideration. First, there should be cover for you to hide in until the doves reach shotgun range. Ideally, you should be able to see approaching doves from every possible direction. You should also be able to swing your gun in a full circle without having to shoot through bushes or trees.

The perfect spot for a blind or island of cover is in a bare, open field so that wherever a dove falls, you will have a good chance of finding it. If you set up on the border of a field and swamp, you'll have to pass up about half the birds that fly into range: that is, you'll be able to recover the birds that fall in the field, but not those that fall in the swamp.

Shoot preferably from a location where you don't have to look in the sun's direction. The background should be as much sky as you can possibly get because a bird silhouettes better against the sky and is easier to see when it is approaching and in shooting range. A dove flying under the level of trees blends in with the background and may become a shadow rather than a silhouette.

Doves usually land into the wind but this has little to do with the direction from which they approach. They can maneuver and turn so quickly that they often wait until the last second to swing into the wind, put their flaps down, and land.

Doves like to land in a bare tree, such as a pecan or walnut, on the edge of a feeding field and look the situation over before landing. Since they are attracted to these observation points, you may want to set up a temporary blind about 20 yards away from the tree. Don't shoot from directly beneath the tree because the limbs can obscure your vision and also break up your shot patterns.

If you use decoys, you must find a bare tree, bush, or fence which is not overgrown with brush so that the decoys will be silhouetted.

Obviously, you will seldom find a spot to shoot from which meets all of these conditions; what you actually do is compromise. The two most important things are to have cover for yourself, and for your shot birds to fall on bare ground or in slight cover where you can quickly find them.

On some large hunts the problem of stand selection is decided for you. The host assigns you to the stand and tells you to stay there, partly for safety and partly to follow hunting party etiquette. If a party is surrounding a field, some shooters will be looking at the sun and others may have large trees nearby which block their vision for certain angles. No one knows where the doves will fly until they start coming in, and some blinds may get a lot of shooting while others get very little.

On most days, patterns of entry and exit develop. Hunters directly under these flight lines get the most action and should be the first to fill their limits. As they leave the field, the considerate host moves other hunters into these hot spots. Some will have moved earlier (after first slipping their chains).

On a farm where some of the crops are planted or managed for dove shooting, the farmer may leave a strip of corn or sunflower standing in the field. The strip, perhaps no more than five or six feet wide, is an almost perfect place to shoot from. There is plenty of cover to hide in, and the strip is surrounded by fallen or cut grain which attracts the birds. When shot, the doves fall on fairly open ground and are reasonably easy to find. The hunter doesn't lose a lot of time looking for downed birds.

With the aid of a machete, a makeshift blind can be put up in a few minutes in an open field, where there will be no trees or groundcover to hinder dove sighting or retrieving. A few leafy branches or stalks of dog fennel can be cut quickly, and the sharp ends pushed into the ground.

Even with a dog along, there are some spots I refuse to consider shooting from, regardless of how many doves might be passing over. Mesquite and cactus clumps can be so dense that a dog will hardly be able to tread his way inside them to find a dove, or if he does, he'll get chewed up with thorns in the process. In the Southeast, several acres of thick kudzu or heavy briars often present an obstacle course not worth the trouble of tackling.

Because of crop rotation, permanent blinds are seldom built for dove shooting. It is unlikely that more than four or five large shoots can be held on a field during one season without running the birds off. This does not justify the elaborate blinds which duck hunters often construct. Temporary blinds are much more suitable and can be built easily and quickly with whatever vegetation is handy.

For early morning shooting, shadows are excellent camouflage. In late afternoon, when doves are on their way to a water hole or roost, shadows replace blinds for most open woods shooting. Naturally, if you are shooting from a large opening where the doves might spot you before they are in range, you should use a low bush for cover.

Much of the success of dove shooting lies in not letting the dove see you until he comes within close enough range for you to make your move to shoot. He may do a few didoes, but he's close enough for you to get off two or three shots. By wearing camouflage, using natural cover in the field, and making a temporary blind, your first shot will often be the first warning to the dove that a hunter is near. If you can fire the first shot before the dove sees you, it will be the easiest shot you have. By the time you

The ideal shooting stand is one in which you can hide, move without being detected, and shoot in all directions.

This strip of cover left by the farmer makes an ideal shooting stand. Hit birds will fall on the bare ground behind or in front of the strip, making recovery easy.

Tops of tall bush are hacked out with machete so that shooter is free to swing and shoot in full circle.

With two doves clearly in range, this hunter tries for a double.

Father-son team uses native vegetation for a blind.

fire your second shot, the bird will be in the midst of aerobatics. Also, with your second and third shot, because of recoil and hunter panic the gun may not be mounted correctly to your cheek and shoulder. Thus, the first shot should be the payoff. The second and third shots are where your shooting average slumps.

One of the most important but difficult things to learn in dove shooting is range estimation. How far away is the bird? Is he in range for the choke?

A flying dove is generally seen as a dark brown or gray shape silhouetted against the sky. You may see some iridescent flecks or light tan breast if the sun strikes the bird right, or you may see the band of white near the tip of the tail when it is spread as a landing flap. Distinctive features, however, are difficult to pick out: you will not see the pink feet tucked up into the feathers, and if you see the eyeballs, the bird is right on top of you.

This dark gray silhouette will be against a white sky on one day, against a dark blue the next, and a little later, against a dark thunderhead. Sometimes you shoot in intense sunlight, but three hours later you may be in a waning light. You hunt in rain and sometimes fog. You squint through dust the first part of the season and perhaps through snowflakes at the last. Sun and wind cut at your eyes and small insects seek sanctuary there. It's no wonder most of us have trouble estimating range, even though we don't need to know exact yardage.

But until you learn to estimate range, you cannot be a good wing shooter or, for that matter, a good sportsman, because you will be lobbing shot at doves far out of effective killing range for your pattern and shot. You might bring one down once in a while with a broken wing, but most of the time you'll be wasting shells or crippling birds which fly off to die a day or two later.

Learning to estimate range takes practice, and you can do this best with aids. To begin, take a yardstick at home, and adjust your pacing stride to one yard so that when you walk off distance in the field you'll be fairly accurate.

Take a minimum of four marker stakes to the field with you. These can be made of wood, but the easiest markers to carry and stick into the ground are made from sections of coathangers. Cut several strips of fluorescent orange fabric about an inch wide and ten inches long, and tie them to the stakes. Put a few extra ribbons in your ammo carrier for tying on weeds, branches, or stumps. Fluorescent or hunter orange is a color which does not occur in nature and is visible under all lighting conditions. The small marker strips, incidentally, will not spook incoming birds.

When you choose a spot to shoot from, or when you build a blind, put your marker stakes in the ground at north, east, south, and west. It's even better if you put them at points in between. The more markers you have as guides, the more accurate your range estimation will be. If you are shooting a modified choke, the stakes should be at 45 yards; with an improved cylinder choke, pace off 35 yards.

Your blind is the center of a circle. The perimeter is an imaginary line running through your markers. Since field conditions vary, you will not be able to put down a stake at every spot you choose, and this is where the extra ribbons come in handy for tying on weeds, fenceposts, or logs (rubber bands and string are helpful in securing the ribbons).

The idea is not to take a shot at any dove unless it flies into your circle. If your stakes are at 45 yards, and if an incoming dove is 20 yards high, when the bird flies over the perimeter, it will be slightly farther away than 45 yards. But you can forget this type of accuracy. We can't take a slide rule to the field to work out each problem. If the bird is 20 yards high and passes your perimeter, by the time you get your gun mounted and swing your shotgun, the dove will be well within range.

While you are sitting there waiting for doves to come in, study the distances to your marker strips. It helps me to visualize distances in 10-yard units the way football fields are marked off. Forty-five yards is a tough shot for any choke on a moving target, especially when combined with the speed and erratic flight of a dove. Sixty yards is half the distance of a football field. I know I cannot shoot accurately at that distance consistently, and I do not try. When a man tells me he kills doves cleanly at 60 or 70 yards, I know he is either a liar, does not know how to measure, injures a lot of birds, or all three.

While marker strips are useful for gauging the range of low-flying doves, estimating the height of trees near your blind will help you determine whether those doves passing above, headed for the next county, are 40 or 80 yards high. You can train your eye to "guestimate" how far above a 50- or 60-foot tree an approaching dove is. You will also, with practice, form a mental picture of what a low-flying dove passing over the stakes at 35 or 45 yards looks like, and this will give you an idea of how high the bird is flying.

To learn range, I have tied birds to limbs and studied them every five yards from 15 to 45 yards. Whenever I take a walk around the block at home, I practice estimating yardage by throwing a baseball, guessing how far it went, then pacing off the distance to see how close I came. I need the practice.

Don't worry if your buddies kid you about your range experiments. If you practice for a month, I will guarantee that you will be able to estimate range better than 90 percent of the other dove shooters you'll meet in the field.

Your range markers will also help you to find doves you knock down. A shot bird seldom falls straight down. The momentum of his flight carries him in the direction he was flying.

If you shoot at only one bird and hit it, keep your eyes on it. Try to mark the exact spot it fell in relation to a nearby weed, cornstalk, or other object. Is it inside or outside your imaginary marker circle?

Do not move your eyes from the spot where the bird lands. Reload your shotgun and walk toward your bird, your eyes still riveted to the spot. When you get there, stop, and look around without moving. If you do not see the bird, hang

When you knock down a dove, especially in dense ground cover, immediately go to the spot where you think the dove fell, and put out a marker such as a handkerchief. You can then work a square-search pattern until you find the bird.

73

a handkerchief or one of your marker ribbons on a weed or drop it on the ground where the wind will not blow it away. Look back toward your stand, take a bearing, and be sure this is where the bird fell.

Search very close to your marker. This is your best bet for finding the bird. If it is injured, it will not move far. It may hide under cover, but usually it squats and holds. If the bird flutters, you will hear and see it. Do not shoot it because you will be too close and blow it up. If you see blood on the wings or a drooping wing or other signs that the bird can't fly, carefully put your gun on grass or other ground cover so you don't get sand in it. Then chase the bird down. Once in a while, a bird will get up and fly off and you'll feel rather foolish. But that's better than chasing and diving at a hobbling bird with a loaded shotgun in your hands. Also, a low flyer may head directly for another blind at head level, and the occupant might not appreciate it if you shoot.

If you cannot find the bird near your marker strip, set up a systematic square search. The worst thing you can do is wander aimlessly. In a few minutes, you won't know where you've looked. Without a marker to keep checking on, I've seen hunters stray off 25 to 35 yards from where a bird fell and spend half an hour looking.

As long as you have put a marker strip down, if another dove flies into range while you are searching for the first, go ahead and shoot. If you fold that one, keep your eye on the spot, go straight to it, and drop another marker strip. Find that one, and then go back and search for your first one.

If a lot of doves are coming in, and you are in the open and spooking them from nearby hunters, you may want to go back to your blind—especially if they're calling you names. When the doves stop coming in, you have your marker to start the search again.

One of the best ways to improve your average of birds per shell expended is to find all the birds you knock down. Yet I'm constantly amazed at hunters who do not use the marker system—or any system. I've seen conscientious sportsmen spend more time at a shoot looking for doves on the ground than for doves in the sky.

If you are being attacked by a wave of doves and tumble the first one you shoot at, you must take your eyes off it in order to get a double or a glorious triple. If you hit a bird with your last shot, you should keep your eye on it until it strikes the ground. Drop a marker strip where you stand, walk to the spot, and drop another strip. When you find the bird, go back to the marker where you performed your outstanding shooting feat. Try to remember exactly where the first bird was falling, make your best guess where it hit, and walk to that spot and drop a marker. You may wish to leave your shooting-spot marker in case you have to come back and take another bearing.

After finding a bird that you did not see fall all the way to the ground, make a point to remember whether you overestimated or underestimated. If there is a consistent pattern, you may be able to correct your estimates, and this will help you to find your birds more quickly. You'll also find that the four to eight range markers you put out at the beginning of the shoot serve as good bearing points. If the dove looked as if it were falling within your shooting perimeter, you won't wander to the next field.

Finding a dove in cover is an art. When you locate one, try to remember what you saw first. Sometimes you will first see the whole dove, but most of the time you will not.

Look for a color that does not seem to belong—that's a little out of place. Sometimes you will see the iridescent sparkle if the sun is on the birds. The light tan of the breast is off-color from most cover. You may first spot an eye or the shape of the head. Sometimes you will see a pink foot or leg. If the tail is spread, you may see the white band of a feather near the tip. I have better luck seeing these distinctive features than the whole dove.

Charley's Principle says that if there is one clump of dense cover in a bare field, that's where a dove will fall. The quicker you can reach the spot where you think the dove fell, the better your recovery percentage. Much of dove hunting is hunting for birds on the ground.

Managing a Hunt

Whether there are 2 gunners or 40 on a dove hunt, someone should be the chief huntsman or boss. The field tactics will be better, and the shooting safer.

It facilitates the shooting if, before entering a field, hunters adopt a standard system of alerting others of approaching doves. Hunters are invariably cooperative in yelling to announce incoming doves; the trouble is there's no method about it.

If 20 hunters are gathered around the border of a harvested milo field, Charley's Principle states that the man with the loudest voice is the one who will first see approaching doves.

He will yell, "Yonder they come!" Well, where do they come from? No one knows! Nineteen necks swivel and crane. Some hunters look high, and others look low; some turn in quick circles, afraid they're missing easy shots, and others look straight up, or into the sun, and develop neck cricks.

A lone dove sneaks in, and the hunter with the foghorn voice shouts, "He's right over you!" and everyone turns frantically trying to spot the intruding target.

If 500 doves filter in all afternoon, the hunter with the loud voice will call every one of them, but he will never give you a clue on direction, bearing, or altitude. After a while, worn out from jerking and turning, you'll ignore him. A little later, after a barrage of vocal blasts, the loud one will come charging down on your stand like a raging bull. "Why ain't you shooting?" he demands. "Doves have been passing all around you."

You reply weakly, "I think I have a whiplash from snapping around all afternoon." Because he is a cousin of the farmer who owns the land, you don't say what you'd like to.

Of course the foghorn is not as bad as the whistler. This character has a weak voice, but he whistles loud. Every time there's a dove within half a mile of the field, he whistles. You rise from your stool, turn a quick circle, and see nothing. Is he whistling at his dog, is there a dove inside the field, or is he just happy?

You see a flock of doves 200 yards high headed for Mexico, and then comes the whistle. Is the whistler letting you know he's on the ball and has seen the high birds, or is he signaling that there are low birds coming in from behind? Has he seen a wildlife officer approaching the field, or has his wife given him a toy whistle for his birthday?

I have never understood why communication in a hunting field should not be clear. Assuming the occupants went through grammar school or were in the Boy Scouts or the military, they must have heard of the compass, know how to tell time, and at least be vaguely aware that a dove is a three-dimensional flyer.

The problem of direction calling should be solved before the shooting starts. There are two systems for doves approaching from outside the field. Others shooting and yelling will let you know when a bird is inside the field perimeter. The center of the field is considered to be the center of a compass. The direction of the dove is announced on the basis of where the dove comes from. If the bird approaches from the north, the hunter who sees it shouts, "Bird, north, low." Another time it might be, "Flock, south, high." This is considerably more specific than "Here they come!"

The Air Force clock system is preferred by some. North is 12 o'clock, east is 3, south is 6; all 12 hours around the clock are used. The announcer shouts, "Three birds, 9 o'clock, high." If he knows the name of the occupant of the stand which the birds will probably fly over, he yells, "Joe, flock, 5 o'clock, low." If the birds are almost on the blind before they are spotted, he may simply call, "5 o'clock, low."

If you are new to dove hunting, you will be surprised at how many birds within range sneak past your blind during a hunt. Even if you have a perfect spot (where you are well hidden but can see in all directions), you can only swing your neck about 180 degrees while sitting. Though you do your best to turn and patrol 360 degrees with your eyes, birds mysteriously come out of nowhere, and are past you before you know it!

Alerts from other hunters are extremely helpful: I'd say that close to half of the doves I shoot at are "called" to my attention by either a shout or a shot.

A calling system should be agreed upon by the hunters before going to the field; this is never an easy task. Unless the landowner or one of the hunters is emphatic about enforcing a system, none will be used and confusion will ensue. Hunters are an independent lot.

Even with only two hunters, perhaps sitting back to back, a calling system helps. The hunter on the approaching side should alert his partner to the dove and an impending shot. The first hunter may very well miss, thereby giving the second hunter a chance. Nothing is more satisfying than knocking down a bird your buddy just missed!

For most hunting, doves should be kept confused and milling about to prevent their landing. Hunters spread out over an area rather than concentrated in areas can usually do this best. For this reason, there is usually only one hunter at a stand. On organized hunts, the landowner or chief huntsman assigns each gunner to a particular spot or stand. If they are surrounding a field the doves have been feeding in, the stands are spaced so as not to leave any wide gaps through which doves will enter and depart.

Another rationale for spacing is in case someone gets careless and shoots a low-flying dove. Shot pellets fired from slightly above the horizontal can injure the eyes of another hunter at 100 yards or more. The experienced huntsman always warns a party not to shoot low under any circumstance, as he knows hunters will be wandering about looking for dead birds and straying to undesignated areas. One hunter cannot keep up with all the others, and for safety's sake all low shooting should be forbidden from the outset.

For several years, twice a season I was invited to hunt with a group of farmers in Georgia. They were fine sportsmen and most of them were outstanding shooters. On my first hunt, at least six or seven of them sidled by, called me off, and said, "Watch out for old Clayton. He's a low shooter."

There were about 20 hunters, and the shoot was well organized. We were driven to blinds surrounding a peanut field, and one by one we hopped out of pickup trucks and took up our

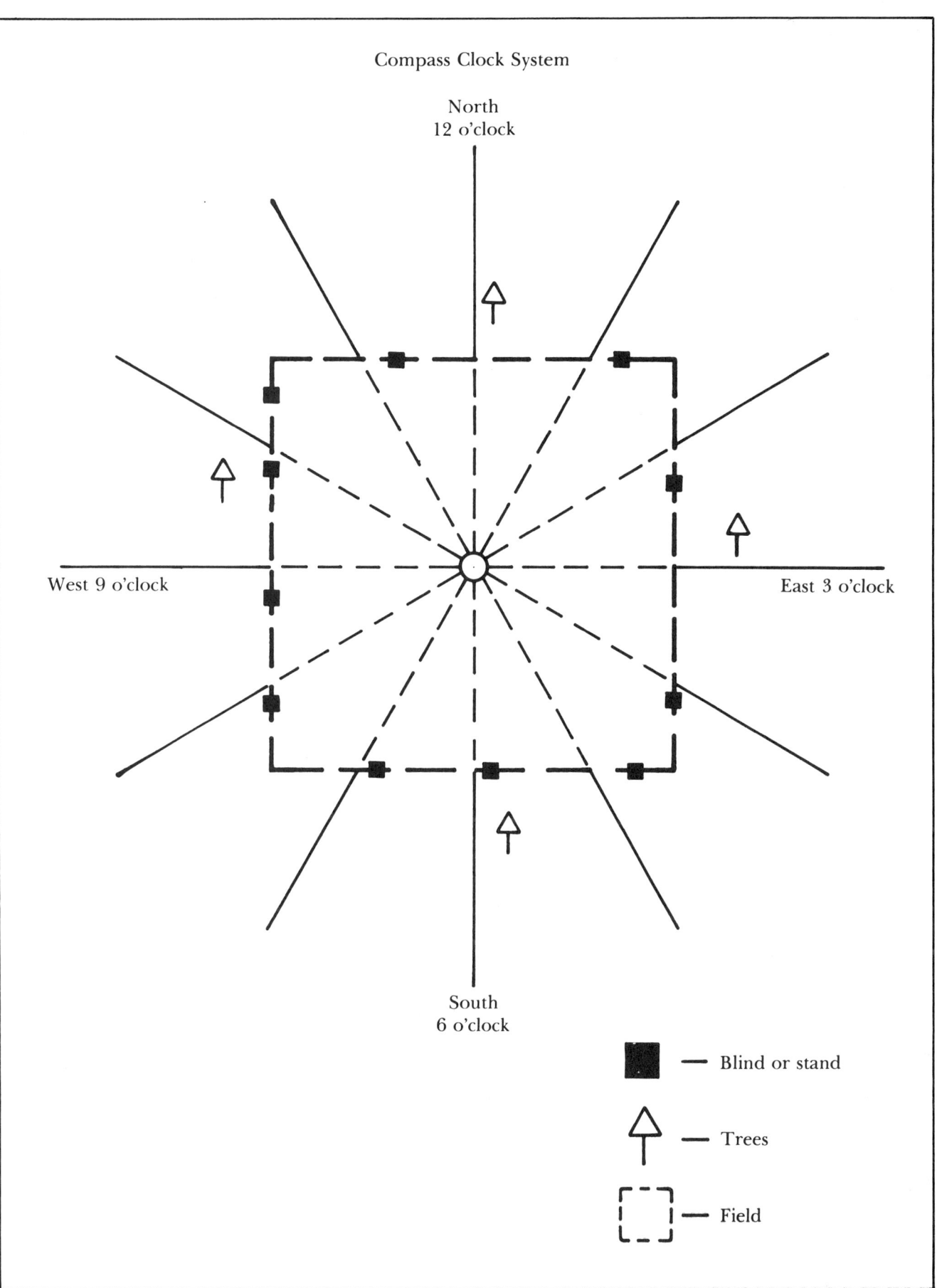

posts. Clayton was two blinds north of me, and I noted his position.

The shooting started slowly about 3:00 p.m. as a few singles and doubles swooped in low in a high wind (doves seem to fly lower when the wind is up). I looked around and noticed the farmer just north of me was moving my way. He came by, smiled, and said, "Clayton is moving. He can't stay still."

Three doves came low out of the middle of the field almost at me. I lowered my gun and then a load of shot cut through the weeds surrounding me. I ducked and waited. I slowly stuck my head up and saw Clayton coming my way carrying his old double shotgun. He hollered, "Did you see where my bird fell?"

I looked at him and replied, "No, but you might check my blind."

I picked up my gear and took off after the farmer who had passed me earlier. I didn't catch him. Then I saw that every hunter in the field was moving. They were all circling and moving to make room and stay ahead of Clayton.

We circled the field twice that afternoon. I didn't shoot too well, as it was difficult to keep one eye on a dove and the other one peeled for Clayton.

During the hunt and the festivities afterwards, all of the farmers made a point of telling me what a great guy Clayton was. Children and dogs loved him, he tithed, and voted the straight Democratic ticket, but he had this one failing: he'd shoot a low dove.

I asked one farmer why they put up with Clayton at the hunts. He looked at me to see if I was kidding, then said, "Didn't you know? Clayton owns the land."

Well, it was an experience, and I looked forward to the hunts each year. I gave Clayton an orange vest, but he wouldn't wear it. Anyway, it wasn't much of a trick learning to stay at least 200 yards away from him.

When there are two hunters at a stand or two decide to sit together when it's a long time between birds, the hunter on the left takes birds flying on the left and the hunter on the right takes birds to the right. For birds flying toward the middle, one of the hunters should call the

Hunter hides behind makeshift blind of dog fennel until dove is within range.

Field borders usually have native cover which provides excellent blinds. When assigned a stand at a large hunt, the shooter should stay there until the hunt manager okays a change.

shot by saying, "You take it," or "My bird." It's fine for the second gunner to back the first provided his muzzle is in a safe place and won't blast the eardrums out of his companion. It is not seemly to lean across another hunter.

When two hunters are together, the one who has the most birds down defers to the other on shooting opportunities. Hunters always help each other mark falling birds and search for hard-to-find birds.

On many dove hunts, you will find yourself with hunters you have not previously met. Questions of house rules, shooting ethics, and safety should be freely and congenially decided on before going to the field.

I have never seen any problem arise over division of the doves after a hunt. However, I have seen hunters blatantly lie about how many shells they shot!

How to Hit a Dove

A sportsman will not shoot a sitting dove. Why? Because he knows before he pulls the trigger that he will kill the bird. There is no challenge to it.

To give the dove a sporting chance, it is shot at on the wing. For most of us, that puts the odds in favor of the dove—about five or six to one.

To readjust those odds, we hunters trick the birds into coming close by using camouflage clothing, decoys, and by hiding behind natural cover or blinds. We hunt in an area frequented by doves so that some are bound to fly our way. We are not after one particular dove—any bird will do. And we use range markers to help us gauge when the doves are at the best range for the shotgun choke we've chosen.

No matter how expert you become with your shotgun, you will never graduate. The challenge will always remain, and the odds will stay with the doves. If you can consistently bag 10 or 12 doves with a box of 25 shells, you are justified in bragging. If, on some glorious day, you knock down 10 straight birds, be reluctant to boast. The very next day it may take you 50 shells to reach a limit. Ten straight birds is about the same as a hole-in-one for golf. You may get lucky and do it, but there is no guarantee of a repeat performance.

For successful shotgunning, your firearm must fit you reasonably well. You must learn to mount it so that the comb of the stock snuggles under your cheekbone and the stock butt melts into your shoulder the same way each time. This causes the barrel to be in the same position relative to your eyes every time, giving you the same image whenever you look down the barrel with both eyes focused on the bird.

Practice dry firing at home with an unloaded

Besides wearing camouflage clothing, hunters use the natural cover of a fencerow to hide from doves until they are in range. With proper timing, doves will be dropped inside the cornfield.

shotgun. Quickly mount your gun, point it at a stationary target such as a light switch, and instantly fire. After you pull the trigger, sight down the barrel as though it were a rifle, and see if you were on the switch. When you can do this perfectly, look two or three yards from the target, say, "Go," and, swinging toward the target, mount your gun. As you pass the target, pull the trigger and keep swinging.

In the field, one of the main causes for missing is that during the excitement of birds diving in, we fail to mount the gun correctly. We are so anxious to hit a dove, and are so afraid of running out of time, that we simply throw up the gun and fire. If the stock is bouncing off your biceps, (instead of being tucked firmly into the shoulder with the comb under the cheekbone), the muzzle cannot possibly be in the proper position. Dry firing should be practiced until you can mount the gun correctly every time without thinking about it, that is, until it becomes a reflex motion. When hunting, your body must be conditioned to the point that your muscles subconsciously move the gun parts to the guide beacons of shoulder and cheek when your mind, free to concentrate on the bird, says, "Now!"

Nearly all outstanding shooters, both shotgunners and riflemen, shoot with both eyes open. This is simply because you see better with two eyes than one, and you need the extra peripheral vision of both eyes to pick up a second and third dove as you fire at the first. If you're a beginning shooter, learn to shoot with both eyes open; if you're used to shooting with one eye closed, it's not difficult to switch to both eyes open.

You can get pointers from reading this book, but you really don't learn how to shoot a shotgun until you take one in hand and start firing it at moving targets. It is surprising how many fathers take their youngsters to a dove field to learn wing shooting. It's about like asking a freshman physics student to build an atom bomb on his first day in class!

It's much easier to learn the fundamentals of hitting a moving target under the controlled

For consistently accurate shooting, the shotgun must be mounted in the same position each time. With practice, this becomes a subconscious motion.

conditions of a skeet or trap field than in the erratic confusion of a hunting field. Although any shotgun handling helps to make a shooter, skeet is better than trap for the budding dove hunter. In trap shooting, the angle at which clay targets are thrown changes with each target and cannot be predicted. However, all of the targets are going-away shots. The dove hunter needs to be able to hit a going-away bird, but this shot is not as common or as difficult as others.

In skeet shooting, there are two trap houses from which clay targets are thrown. The high-house bird is thrown at the same angle each time; it is higher than the target from the other house. The low-house bird is thrown at the same angle each time; it sails lower than the bird from the high house but over the same stake in the outer center of the field. The target angle is changed by the shooters themselves moving to eight different stations. The hunter learns to shoot straight-away targets at stations 1 and 7. On the other stations, he gets a variety of deflection shots which he will encounter in the field.

Skeet is ideal practice for the beginning dove shooter. Once he can consistently break targets from stations 4 and 8, he is over the hump. These two angles are the big bugaboos for new dove hunters (or for old-timers if they're out of practice).

When you shoot with a rifle at a still target, you aim. When you shoot with a shotgun at a moving target, you point. You have an expanding pattern, and you do not have to center the target. If you aim at a moving target, you will shoot behind it; because of the target's speed, your reaction time, and the time it takes for your shot to travel, your pattern will cross the path of where the target used to be. For your shot to intersect the moving target, you must lead it. Lead is handled by swinging the barrel from behind the target until it catches up with and passes the target, pulling the trigger, and continuing the swing in a follow-through.

It is difficult to explain lead to a new student because he wants you to tell him how many feet to lead a bird. Since the angles of approaching doves are never the same, and two shooters do not swing a gun at the same speed, no pat answer in feet is possible. In a dove field, there is no time to take a calculator and plot the angle and speed

Trap Shooting

Skeet Shooting

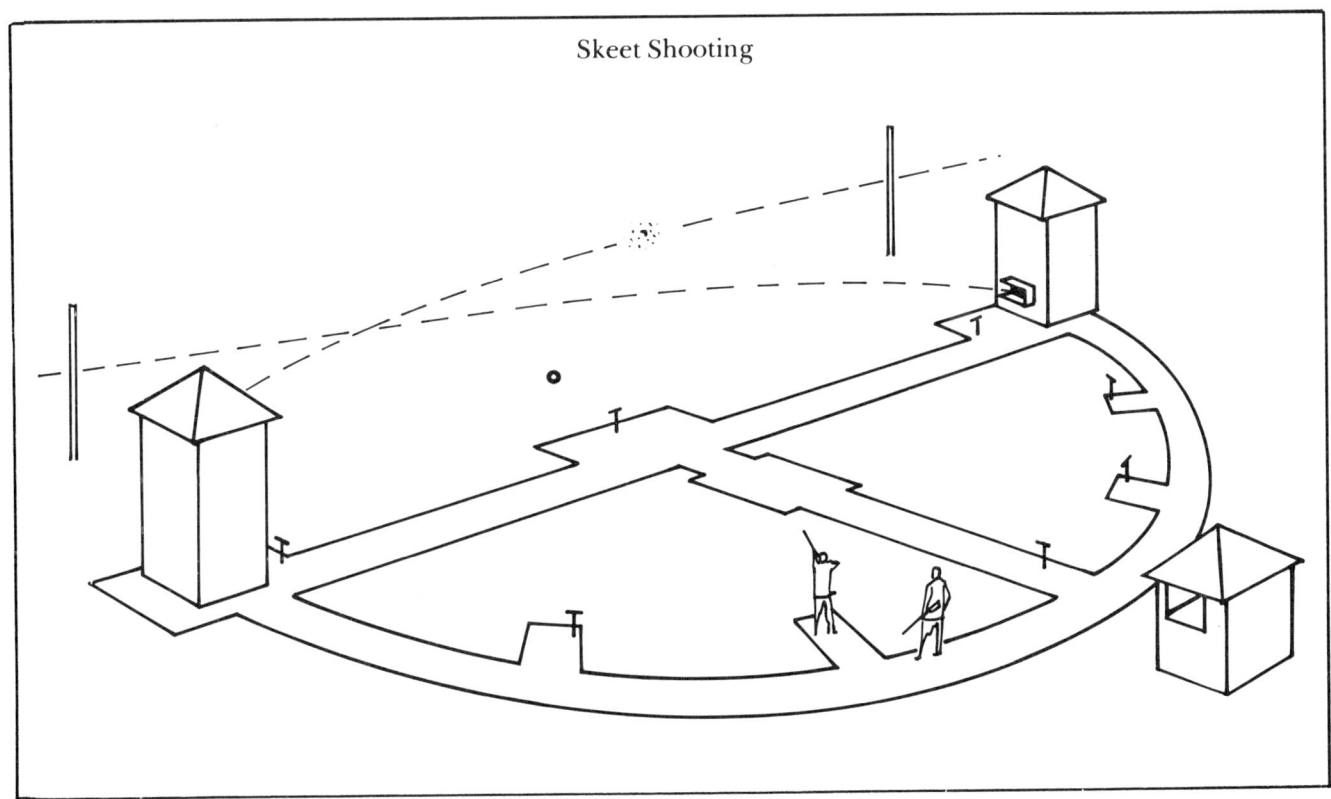

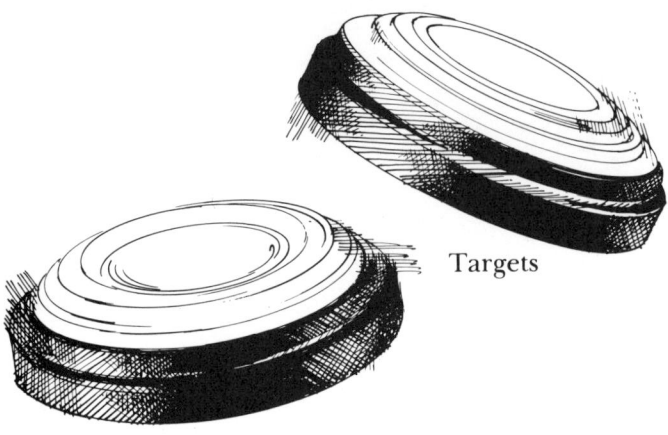
Targets

of a dove. The easiest way to learn to lead a target is by trial and error on a skeet field. If you broke the target, you led correctly. If you missed, you probably shot behind.

The number 4 skeet station is almost a 90-degree deflection shot. You are at right angles to the path of the clay target. Ninety degrees is the maximum amount of deflection, or lead, you can have. It requires the most lead of any angle because the target passes across the path of your shot cone faster than at any other angle. The opposite extreme is the theoretical target thrown perfectly level with no angle straight away from you. Once you pointed your muzzle at that target, it would be on target no matter how far out the target traveled.

The number 8 skeet station is confusing for the brand-new shooter. The birds are thrown a little higher than his head and almost directly at him. They are incomers. He has but the briefest time to shoot, and by the time his eyes define the target, his muzzle is behind it. He swings along the path of the target, catches the target and blacks it out with his muzzle, pulling the trigger and continuing to swing along the target path. If he breaks the target, he did not see it when he pulled the trigger.

The incoming dove is the toughest shot for a

Clay target shooting with a practice trap pays off in better field shooting.

Approaching doves abruptly turn as hunter rises from hiding place to shoot.

beginner to make, but it is the most frequent shot he will get. He hunts from a stand or blind and most of the shots are birds coming toward him. Even a hunter exerienced on other game has trouble with incoming doves. Why shouldn't he? Most of his field experience has been on game going away from the hunter—grouse, woodcock, quail, pheasant, or rabbit.

The incoming clay target on station 8 wraps the new shooter up in knots. Then all of a sudden he breaks one and understands what he's doing. It's suddenly duck soup—the easiest target on the field. Very quickly he is able to stand at that station and break 20 out of 25 targets. Old-timers can do it blindfolded—swinging their guns with the sound of the trap throwing the bird.

It is quicker and cheaper to learn how to hit a moving target on a skeet field than in a dove field. Clay targets from all eight stations are similar to dove angles you will get when hunting. If a skeet club does not have a waiting line of shooters, the manager will probably let you concentrate on key stations such as 4 and 8.

Let the manager know if you are inexperienced in clay target shooting, so he can check you out on safety and etiquette. There's always a skeet veteran around who'll help you get started on such matters as the correct stance; it's the same for both dove and skeet shooting. You stand flat-footed with feet spread and an equal amount of weight on each foot. Your feet are spread enough so that you can easily swivel at the hips to allow your gun to swing in a 180-degree arc. A right-handed shooter breaks his left knee slightly and leans forward. The main thing in a shooting stance is, of course, that you are balanced and comfortable.

When you begin hunting doves, you'll want to shoot from a standing position. Some hunters seem to shoot almost as well sitting on their

stools as standing. I can't and gave up trying a long time ago. One reason is the pure physics of it. My body does not swing as easily sitting down as standing. Secondly, I've always practiced from a standing position and do not mind the extra exertion of rising from my stool.

There is one thing at a skeet field you should do differently from the other shooters. Liberalized skeet rules allow the gunner to call for the target with his gun fully mounted. You should call for your bird with the gun stock either at your hip or half-mounted. At the sound of the trap, before you see the target, you start to mount your gun. This is in preparation for the way you'll do it in the field; most of the time you will mount your gun when you see a dove crossing your marker stakes, although sometimes you will hear a sneaky one from behind before you see it.

The other skeet shooters will insist that you mount your gun before you call for the bird, that you are handicapping yourself by not doing so. Firmly tell them that you are practicing for the dove field and not for competitive skeet shooting. Learning and practicing mounting your gun properly when a target sails out is as important as anything else you will learn. You do not always see a dove early. Many scoot by and are almost out of range before you see them. You barely have time to mount your gun and fire one shot before they are gone.

There are many hilarious stories of expert skeeters going to the dove field for the first time. There is nothing a field shooter would rather see than a city skeeter get his comeuppance. I once took a middle-aged skeet shooter on his first dove hunt. He consistently averaged 92 out of 100 in skeet. Halfway through the hunt, I returned to the car for a drink of water. I heard a strange sound and went around to the other side of the car and found my friend blubbering. It seems that he had shot two boxes of shells and had not cut a feather. I did what any normal hunter would have done under the circumstances—I rolled on the ground in grateful glee!

I also blackmailed him into contributing several fishing lures to my tackle box under threat of telling the story all over town. Of course, I knew I could not collect for long. A good skeet shooter may have a little trouble converting from clay targets to doves, but it doesn't take him long to learn the difference. Let him get a few dove hunts under his belt, and he'll make the country boys take notice.

Ideally, a hunter should be able to break 16 or 17 clay targets out of 25 before going to the field. Ten sessions on the skeet field, and he'll probably be able to do it. Look at it this way. If you can't hit a target when you know beforehand where it's going, how do you expect to hit a darting dove when even the bird itself doesn't know where it's going?

If you are not conveniently located to a skeet or trap field, one solution is to go in with a buddy and buy a practice trap for about $40.00. The springs on practice traps can be jiggered to

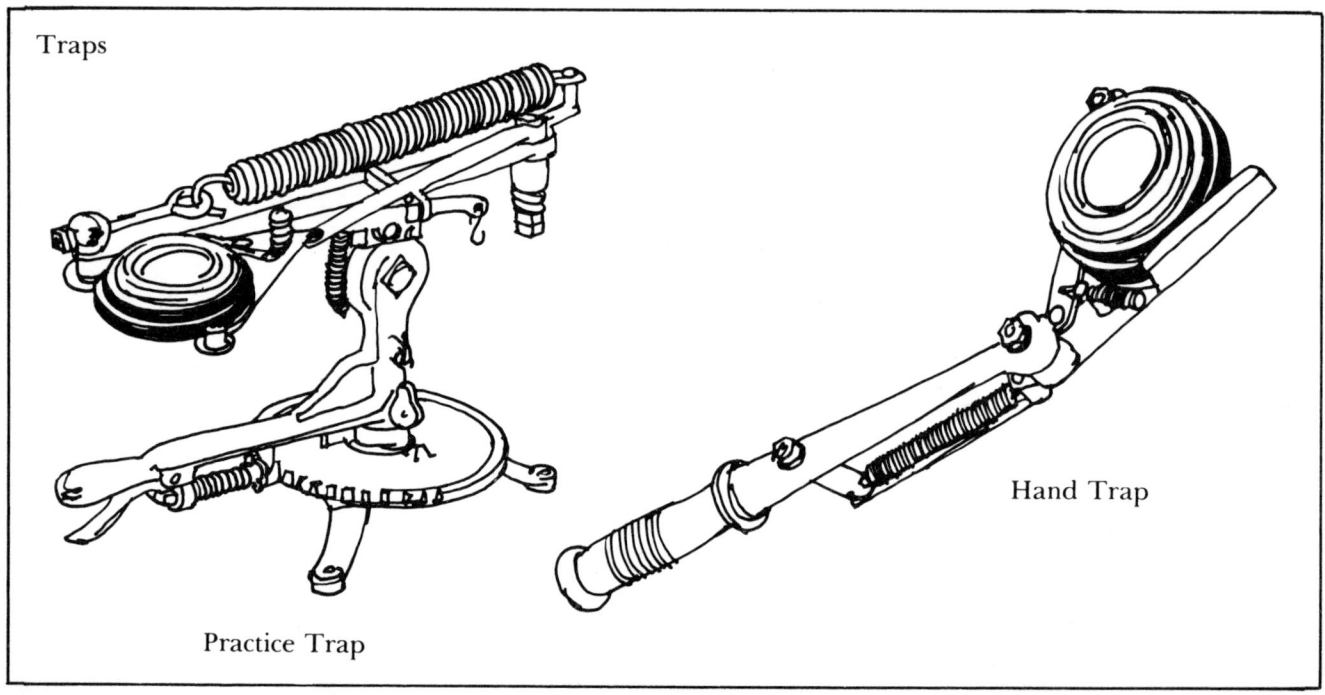

Traps

Practice Trap

Hand Trap

throw a target as fast as a dove flies. The operator can also change the angle to keep the shooter guessing.

The best place to mount the trap is high off the ground, perhaps on an old building. The operator should be protected by a shield of plywood. The direction in which shots might be fired should be safe for 200 yards.

The shooter moves around to take targets of different angles. He should practice a great deal on high targets thrown over his head as he faces the trap. To understand deflection, or lead, more quickly, he should stand back at an angle of 90 degrees from the target flight path and practice on these maximum-lead targets.

The shooter and the trap operator alternate, and practice should be taken as simulated dove shooting and not a playful game of who can break the most targets. It is important to find out what stance is comfortable for you. Again, as in skeet shooting, the gun should not be mounted to the shoulder and cheek until you see the bird or hear the trap. The swing of the barrel, starting from behind the bird, starts as you are mounting the gun. Both eyes are open and are focused on the target. Swing smoothly to catch up with the target; as you pass it and pull ahead with your muzzle, pull the trigger and keep swinging. Don't jerk your head up when you pull the trigger—you can see whether the bird breaks without doing this. Keep the gun cheeked tightly when you pull the trigger, and follow through with your swing.

If you don't want to buy a practice trap, you can buy a hand trap for about $8.00 and soon learn to throw clay targets fairly accurately. Team up with a friend or two for this and alternate throwing and shooting. Before you practice, be sure to set up safety rules so that no one points a shotgun toward the target thrower.

Targets with a hand trap should be thrown with a variety of angles to simulate doves. The emphasis should be on targets which are incomers to the shooter and at 90 degrees from the way he is facing.

Practice traps, hand traps and clay targets are available through sporting goods dealers. Your dealer will know also the locations of the nearest skeet or trap fields.

Domestic pigeons are not classified as game birds. However, a flock which has been shot at is plenty wild, and often the best practice you can get for doves or bandtails. Domestic pigeons, sometimes called rock pigeons, damage farmers' barns and destroy crops when their numbers build up. Some farmers are anxious to have their flocks reduced and will gladly let you hunt if you convince them you won't shoot the eaves off their barns.

Before shooting pigeons, be sure you know the local laws about discharging firearms. Big flocks sometimes fly in and out of cities, and it is not a good idea to shoot if there are people nearby who will become upset. Although there is no season on domestic pigeons, they should not be shot during the mating season unless they have become a nuisance or a sanitation problem.

Domestic pigeons work well to decoys and are ideal for training dogs to retrieve. I make it a point never to shoot at a lone pigeon which looks as though it's going crosscountry. It might be someone's homing or racing pigeon.

I have never had any trouble finding someone who wants to cook domestic pigeons I have shot. In fact, I've served them as bandtails and the guests never knew the difference. I once served them as "small ducks" and one hunter complained that his tasted fishy!

More on Shooting

It's easy to hit a flying dove in theory. All you do is mount your shotgun when the bird is in range, start swinging your muzzle from behind the dove, overtake the bird along its flight path, swing past it, pull the trigger, and keep swinging. The entire ballet is smoothly enacted in no more than one second. For the finale, you walk out onto the field and pick up your bird.

The theory is simplicity itself—it's the execution that makes mortals of us all, that is, causes our blood pressures to rise and our tempers to fray and impels us to repeat words we've seen written on restroom walls.

Before we go farther, let me clarify one point. It is not difficult to "start swinging your muzzle from behind the dove." The bird is moving from 50 to 60 feet a second. As you raise your gun stock to your shoulder and cheek, with both eyes focused on the target, you begin to swing the barrel along the flight path. In this brief instant, the dove will get ahead of your muzzle. At its speed, it can hardly help doing so.

From the instant the dove passes your range marker and you decide to shoot, the entire sequence of movement is smooth and positive with no stopping—from mounting your shotgun to pulling the trigger and following through with your swing. Your eyes are focused on one bird, the one you intend to acquire, no matter how large the flock. You must make a decision and stick to one bird. You are not allowed to balk—that is, if you want to take birds home.

Your shotgun is mounted while your eyes are glued to one bird. The gun must be instantly and snugly mounted in the same position each time. That is why practice mounting and dry firing at home improves your shooting. You rehearse and rehearse until your subconscious and body muscles learn to guide the stock to the same cheek and shoulder position every time.

At this point, you may well be wondering how your mind will think through all of these movements in one second. This is where instinctive shooting, the art of letting your trained subconscious take over and react for you, comes in.

Although the conscious mind can go rapidly from thought to thought, it can handle only one particular thought at any given fraction of a second. The subconscious mind, however, is a control panel capable of handling many functions at the same time—a memory computer which can be programmed.

To illustrate the workings of the two, think of the performance of a saxaphone player. At a given instant, he is blowing through a reeded mouthpiece, working ten fingers, tapping a foot, swaying to the music, and staring at a blonde in the audience. His conscious mind may be focusing on the blonde—but the music goes on controlled by his subconscious mind. It has been imprinted through practice.

It is not possible for a sax player to simultaneously and consciously think through each operation of moving ten fingers, controlling his breath and the reed, patting his foot, and swaying his body. If his playing depended on thinking through each step, he could move only one key at a time, and he'd lose that when his attention reverted to the blonde.

The same is true in dove shooting. Time is

If you see incoming doves while you're in the open, hold still and chances are they'll come on in. If you squat to hide, the movement will give you away and the doves will flare.

Author quickly reloads shotgun after flurry of shooting. With one quick move, he can stand up, raise gun, and shoot from balanced foot position. Even if dove sees him and jinks, the birds will not be able to get out of range before author fires one or two shells.

critical: the conscious mind cannot control the bodily functions of mounting the gun, focusing the eyes on the bird, and swinging the barrel while working the mathematics of intersecting a bird flying at 55 feet per second at an angle of 70 degrees with a shot string traveling at 1,200 feet per second.

The subconscious computer can handle the problem easily if it has been imprinted by practice shooting at clay targets, domestic pigeons, doves, and other winged game. It records hits and misses and makes corrections submitted by the conscious mind. It can be influenced by your will.

You quickly learn that the main reason a beginner misses a clay target or a dove is that variable called lead. If you do not lead enough, your shot string passes behind the target. Lead is controlled by two factors—how fast you swing your gun and how far in front of the bird your muzzle is when you pull the trigger. We assume that your gun was mounted correctly, that you did not raise your head when you pulled the trigger, and that you followed through with the shotgun swing. These three factors are easy to computerize into your subconscious with practice.

If you consciously know that you are shooting behind targets, then your conscious mind should say, "Subconscious, I *will* you to pull the trigger when the muzzle is farther in front of the bird." When you hit the next target, your subconscious will tape the action. The tape will be imprinted more deeply if you consciously review the steps, remembering what you can, and tell the subconscious that that is the way it is done. The more successful imprints you make, the better the subconscious replays for similar shots in the future. Confidence and success oil the subconscious machinery.

In the previous chapter, you may have wondered why I so strongly recommend skeet for the beginning wing shooter. In skeet shooting, the conditions are controlled—it is easy to get an old-timer to stand behind you and tell you why you missed, and you can consciously make corrections. The first few rounds you shoot will have to be handled by your conscious because you don't yet have an imprinted tape for your subconscious. Your conscious shooting will be jerky and erratic but you will hit some targets and the information will be recorded. As you learn to relax and let your subconscious take over, your swing will smooth out, and you will break more targets.

It's much more difficult for the beginner to learn in a dove field because when he misses he doesn't know what he's doing wrong. From what he's heard from other shooters, he suspects he's not leading the birds enough. However, it's hard for him to grasp how far ahead he should swing the gun before pulling the trigger. In addition, there's nothing controlled about a dove field. Every bird comes in differently. The more he misses, the more discouraged he becomes. There's little good input into his computer.

On a skeet field, the beginner learns to shoot incomers, straightaways, and targets with deflections of 30, 60 and 90 degrees, which brackets all of the angles the dove shooter will ever get. His subconscious must interpolate between these angles but his tape has some basic data to start with. The field angles may look a little cockeyed, but they're merely variations of skeet targets. Whether the bird dives, zooms up, or flies level, the hunter must still swing from behind along the flight path of the bird, pass the bird, pull the trigger, and keep swinging.

You can determine how far ahead your muzzle should be when you pull the trigger only by trial and error. When you fold a dove, review the process in your conscious mind, and impress it upon your subconscious. The subconscious thrives on success and compliments.

Very few hunters miss doves because they shoot too far ahead. Most misses are caused by shooting behind birds.

Instinctive shooting, to reiterate, is letting the subconscious take over the controls. The conscious constantly tries to dominate things, making it hard for you to relax and let the subconscious operate. The more you rely on the subconscious for a given action, the more easily you will do it. With practice, you can increase your subconscious control time.

Less conscious thought and more subconscious control generally results in better shooting. To illustrate the evils of too much conscious thought, suppose you are at a dove stand and have put out range markers. You look at the horizon and see a dove 400 yards away headed straight for you, and decide that the bird will fly directly over your stand. You begin to think about its height and speed and how far you will lead it. You have plenty of time, and you spend it thinking about exactly how you will handle the shot. To make sure of your shot, you mount your gun and begin tracking the dove when your target is still 75 yards away. Your mind flits back to lead; you swing ahead of the bird, decide to shoot, remember your range marker and lower your gun. The bird is over your marker, you think about your lead, mount your gun, remind yourself to swing through the bird, pull ahead 10 feet, stop the gun, pull the trigger, and miss.

As Fred Moses looks on, author waits until dove crosses his range marker and then makes a positive move to shoot.

As author straightens up, with both eyes focused on the dove, he begins raising the stock of the shotgun to his cheek, keeping muzzle high to track the bird's flight path.

With both feet firmly planted on the ground, author is balanced to shoot. As the comb of the stock nears his cheekbone, with stock butt going into the shoulder V, the muzzle is swinging to catch up with zig-zagging dove.

The shotgun is firmly nestled into the same firing position it has gone into thousands of times before. The author's eyes have never left the dove. Well-balanced, he swings the muzzle, and as it passes the dove he pulls the trigger and keeps swinging the barrel. This sequence of four steps took less than one second.

Hunter rises out of the palmetto to swing toward a pair of mourning doves swooping in low.

You've thought yourself right out of an easy shot! Your controls were on conscious, and your conscious tripped you up.

Allow me to cover a couple of points before we discuss how the incomer should be handled. Whenever you are hunting doves, never, never click your shotgun safety off until you are mounting the gun to shoot. Range markers are put out not only as a guide for the choke you are shooting but as a beacon to switch from conscious to subconscious controls.

Now, you see the dove at 400 yards flying directly toward you. Do not allow your conscious mind to dwell on any of the technicalities of shooting. Do not think of your shooting average or how many straight birds you've shot. Do not plot in your conscious mind how you will handle the shot. (When my conscious mind insists on thinking about lead, I force it to think how cold I'd be if I were sitting naked on an iceberg. I try to relax and almost ignore the approaching dove.)

In other words, force yourself not to think about the dove or make a move until it crosses the range marker. Then, in one continuous move as both eyes focus on the bird, click the safety off as the gun is mounted, and begin to swing the barrel from behind the dove. Following its path, overtake the bird by swinging the muzzle, and as you pass ahead of the bird, pull the trigger and follow through with the swing. If you are relaxed, all of these steps will follow smoothly upon each other in one second.

In trying to reconstruct the steps after shooting, you will probably not recall snapping the safety off, mounting the gun, swinging the gun, or following through. I always remember the pointing picture as the trigger is pulled, however.

In the field, you will have many shots in which all of the above is completed in less than a second when an unexpected dove suddenly darts by. After these fast shots, I cannot recall any of the steps including the pointing picture, although I may fold the bird. In fact, some of the best shots any hunter makes are pure instinct with no time to think.

Learn to make your moves in a quick and positive, not panicky, manner. You can rush off a shot too soon before the muzzle ever catches up with a dove. A big advantage of range markers is that there need be no balking while you wonder if the bird is in range. Except for very high birds, you will know the dove is in range and can instantly make the decision to shoot when it crosses your markers.

The following description of sighting and shooting a bird will illustrate why he who hesitates in dove hunting is lost. Let's say you are shooting a modified choke, your range markers are at 45 yards, and a dove is flying directly toward you at 40 miles an hour and crosses the marker 15 yards high. This means the bird is closing in on you at 20 yards a second, and flying across your marker about 15 yards high. Your first shot should be now. The angle between your gun and the ground is about 30 or 35 degrees when you shoot. You miss.

At the rate the bird is closing, you do well to fire the second shot when the bird is at an angle of 60 or 65 degrees. You miss. By the time you swing past the bird for the third shot, you will be firing at an angle of 90 or 95 degrees, straight up. You can't shoot much past 100 degrees unless you are a contortionist or unless you turn around.

Thus, you have had three good shots at the bird. Even if you missed all three times, you handled the opportunity properly. On days when birds are scarce, you want to take every opportunity at birds in range for your choke.

Let's take the same approaching problem again; but this time there are three birds—your chance to make a triple and be a hero. If you pussyfoot around when the doves cross your marker, you won't get your first shot off until the birds are at an angle of 50 or 60 degrees. You may get your second round off, but you'll never fire the third.

If you train yourself not to make a move until the bird crosses your marker perimeter, it will improve your instinctive shooting. You know you have to shoot rapidly, and your subconscious will take over. In addition, if you don't move until the birds cross, you will not be spooking them out of range.

Don't worry about losing time if you are sitting on a shooting stool. As you stand up, you will be clicking off the safety, mounting the gun, and starting to swing your barrel from behind the dove. Once up, you can continue to swing, pass the bird, pull the trigger, and keep swinging.

If it's all that easy, you may be thinking, why can't a hunter shoot 10 straight birds day after day? He can't for the same reason that Hank Aaron can't hit a home run every time he goes to the plate, and we all agree that Hank knows what he's doing when it's his turn at bat. He keeps his eyes on the ball, makes an instant decision to swing, and his subconscious controls move the bat forward. Sometimes he puts it all together and the ball goes over the fence for another record; other times he only cuts a lot of air.

Sometimes the extra dido the pitcher puts on the ball makes Hank miss—the same way a jinking dove will throw you off the instant you pull the trigger. However, I do not think these occasional antics account for a lot of missed doves. When a dove hunter goes out into the field, he's simply playing in the majors—trying to perform a difficult feat. If he bats .333, he's doing fine. That's just the nature of the game.

The formidable reputation of the dove's speed and aerobatics is one of its best defenses. While driving to a field, conversation centers mainly around the difficulty of hitting doves. As the hunters head for their stands, there is much friendly banter about missing. Even when the field is swarming with birds, a buddy will stop shooting and ask if you are shooting blanks or if you need more shells. When you miss, someone is always watching. The one who sees your debacle is never hesitant about broadcasting it. There are no secrets on a dove hunt.

Dove lore is filled with tales about the ones that got away, and you can become infected by this pessimistic outlook. If you are not careful, your buddies will talk you into ruin, and you will think yourself into disaster.

Johnny Mercer, the Hollywood song writer, has the answer in one of his songs, "You got to accentuate the positive, eliminate the negative."

Dove hunting is like shooting craps. If you don't believe you're going to win, you better stay out of the game.

Think positively, and your subconscious will respond accordingly. If you're going to hunt doves, you gotta believe!

How Hunting Regulations are Set

All fish and wildlife found within the United States are owned by the American people. The authority to manage wildlife in each state is delegated to a state agency by the state legislature or constitution. Each state game and fish department holds the wildlife in trust for the people and is responsible for its welfare.

Wildlife is a renewable resource. Since a percentage of it can be harvested without endangering the breeding population, hunters are allowed to crop the wildlife. In fact, hunting is often a tool of wildlife management to keep populations in balance with habitat. Wildlife cannot be stockpiled, especially such short-lived species as mourning doves, whitewings, and bandtails.

The annual harvest is controlled by length of hunting season, manner of taking, shooting hours, daily limits, and possession limits. Each state agency has an enforcement section to encourage outdoorsmen to obey state and federal laws.

Since migratory birds—waterfowl, doves, wild pigeons, woodcock, snipe, gallinules, and coots—move freely across state lines, Congress has given the authority to manage these species on behalf of the people to the Department of the Interior. The Fish and Wildlife Service, a division of the Interior, handles the management.

Migrating birds, of course, don't care about state and national boundaries, but the public, wildlife agencies, and hunters do. Migratory birds are recognized as an international resource requiring conservation on a continental basis. Protection of migratory birds on the North American continent is provided for by conventions between the United States and Great Britain (for Canada), concluded in 1916, and between the United States and the United Mexican States, concluded in 1936. Protection in the United States is provided by the Migratory Bird Treaty Act of 1918. This act makes hunting, killing, selling, purchasing, or possessing migratory birds unlawful except as permitted by the Secretary of the Interior.

The following general statement from the Department of the Interior explains how regulations are set. "The Secretary of the Interior annually adopts hunting regulations to permit a reasonable harvest of migratory game birds and to leave an adequate breeding stock for subsequent years. To provide a sound basis for the regulations, considerable information is assembled each year on current populations of birds and on numbers available for harvesting. With a year's accumulation of data, the Secretary sets up a framework of proposed hunting regulations, including season lengths, bag and possession limits, and the earliest opening and latest closing dates within which the State game departments recommend hunting seasons best suited to conditions in their States."

Within the framework allowed by the Department of the Interior, individual states are given certain options to meet their conditions. For instance, a state which knows its doves will migrate early naturally chooses the earliest season opening permitted by the federal framework. A state may choose a split season, the first part to allow hunting for doves raised locally before they migrate and the second part for any birds which have remained or migrated in.

The states are allowed to make laws or regulations more restrictive than the Department of the Interior's regulations, but not more liberal. Furthermore, laws provide that hunting can be stopped in season if unusual weather or disease takes an undue toll of birds.

The welfare of the birds as a whole is always considered first. Secondly, the harvest of doves and wild pigeons must be regulated so that the hunters in each state have a fair chance to harvest an equitable number. Since doves, whitewings, and bandtails migrate to Mexico, the treaty with this nation must be considered as their hunters are also entitled to a percentage of the harvest. Canada also has an interest because it produces a small percentage of bandtails and mourning doves.

On August 31 of an average year, there are about 500 million mourning doves in the United States, according to James L. Ruos, Chief of Dove Surveys, Office of Migratory Bird Management, Fish and Wildlife Service. The season opens the next day in many states. Hunters will spend about 11.6 million recreational days in pursuit of doves.

Long before the season opens, the Fish and

Jump shooting in New Mexico. (Photo credit: New Mexico Department of Game and Fish)

Television and movie actor Robert Fuller is happy with this white-winged dove bagged near El Centro, California.

Wildlife Service and the state wildlife agencies face the formidable task of setting hunting regulations which will allow hunters an equal chance to harvest the birds, but which will in no way endanger the breeding population for the following spring. To the eternal credit of these agencies, they have succeeded in doing it. Statistics show that the annual hunting take has little or no effect on the total population the following autumn. And, miracle of miracles, nearly all of the hunters are satisfied with the length of the seasons and the bag limits!

The wildlife agencies have accomplished this because of the tremendous amount of research that has been done on the life history of the mourning dove. Wildlife biology is not an exact science, but biologists have accumulated enough data to base their regulation proposals on sound information.

For many years, doves have been banded so that migration populations and routes could be understood. Since only three or four bands out of every 100 doves banded are returned, the studies have been slow and tedious. (It is highly important for continuing research that hunters return bands to the appropriate address, including the date and location where the bird was taken.)

One of the major breakthroughs in banding studies revealed the importance of establishing three management units for the continental United States. An average of 95 percent of each of the three management units' hunting kill is produced within the unit. As populations may vary between units, obviously each unit may need different seasons and limits. Banding and other studies also showed the possibility of zoning within a state to vary season times.

Since 1954, call-count surveys on close to 800 routes have been made each year at the height of the breeding season to learn population indices. Based on statistical analysis, a reasonable estimate can be made of the number of doves there will be on August 31—a time of peak population and immediately prior to the opening of the hunting season.

State and federal surveys are made after the hunting season to determine the number of birds killed, the number of hunters, number of birds bagged by each hunter, and other statistics. With the pooling and accumulation of this data, and the use of modern computing machines, the Fish and Wildlife Service compiles a great amount of information on which to base regulations.

The call-count surveys each spring indicate the population expected. Other studies show how many hunters there are and what they may be expected to bag under given regulations. The experts then work back to determine a proposed regulation framework for each of the three management units. Before the regulations are finalized, the state agencies and conservation organizations are consulted. For the 1975–76 season, the public also was asked to comment on federal guidelines in the preparatory stage.

Let's look at the results of this system.

Composite statistics for a recent hunting season show that the season opened with 500 million doves in the United States. Roughly 50 million were harvested and the crippling loss was estimated at 13.7 million. The total birds killed would represent 12.7 percent of the total United States flock. As biologists have long known that doves have a 65–80 percent annual mortality whether they are hunted or not, it is apparent that the 12.7 percent taken by hunters has little or no effect on the dove population for the coming year. In fact, it is a modest percentage, "set" well on the conservative side for the dove population in case of unpredictable hazards such as early freezes and disease.

Of the continental 48 states, 31 have mourning dove seasons. You may well ask why the remaining 17 do not, especially if you live in one

of them. There is no biological reason. Ruos says, "All states currently closed to dove hunting could provide hunting opportunities in the future without jeopardizing the population. The potential for dove hunting would be greatest in Nebraska, North Dakota, South Dakota, Indiana, and Ohio."

In some of the states closed to dove hunting, the bird has been removed from the game list and classified as a songbird. There is an increasing number of citizenry and organizations which oppose all hunting, and they have let their feelings be known to the state legislatures. Their opinions are based on emotional reaction and not biological fact, but, nevertheless, they are becoming more powerful.

Hunters in dove hunting states are happy to receive migrating birds from the nonhunting states. They are glad for the chance to harvest a renewable resource, and view conservation as the wise *use* of natural resources.

In many states, legal dove shooting begins 30 minutes before sunrise.

Field Care, Dressing, and Recipes

Too many hunters worry needlessly about shot doves spoiling in the field or on the drive home, especially during September when the weather can be uncomfortably warm. With minimal care, the birds will do fine. I've never had any problem, even when hunting the San Joaquin and Imperial Valleys of California where the mercury often goes to 110°.

Morning or afternoon shooting periods seldom last more than two or three hours. If you dress your doves at the end of either session, they won't have been dead long enough to ripen. On the drive home, guard against storing them in a hot car trunk for long. If you don't have an ice chest for the trunk, move the doves up front with the passengers.

The ideal way to handle doves, of course, would be to shoot them in the front yard of a poultry processing plant. Then you could rush inside with a freshly killed dove, hang it by its feet, decapitate it, and let the blood run. After skinning and eviserating the dove, you'd put it in iced water to bring the body temperature to below 40°, and you'd then either keep the bird iced or go ahead and freeze it.

Doves knocked down in the field, however, present too messy a problem to bleed. Blood and feathers invariably stick together on your hands and then on your face, gun, and clothes as though you've been tarred and feathered.

When the shooting slows, I've seen old-timers who'd wait for the next flight by picking or skinning a bird. That's not for me! If I plan to drive home that evening, I wait until I can get near such conveniences as hot water. If I'm spending the night locally, I dress the birds in the field when the shoot is over and hope I can find a nearby creek to wash the dressed birds and myself.

While the shooting is going on, I pick up my birds and try to store them in a shady spot above ground so they'll be aerated—that's about all that is practical or necessary. I have enough problems trying to hit another bird without worrying about the finer points of processing.

If you make the mistake of storing your doves on shady grass, you'll have to keep checking to make sure that a Labrador retriever doesn't find one and take it to his master! I've accused several Lab owners of specifically training their dogs to swipe birds!

If you're moving around the field, you may want to carry your birds with you in a shooting vest, canvas storage bag under your shooting stool, or mesh bag made for toting. On a very hot day, doves should not be stored too long in a surplus GI metal ammo box. They need ventilation, not cooking.

It's quick and easy to dress a limit of doves, and I don't mind it; I just prefer to do it all at

Doves stored in the game bag of canvas shooting stool will not spoil before hunt is over. It's easier to clean all your birds at one time when you're through hunting for the day.

one time, so that I get messy only once. When it's necessary to clean doves in the field, be careful about littering. I once ran into about 30 hunters dressing their limits who were making the field look like a poultry plant that had blown up—small wonder that farmers post their lands!

A huge plastic garbage bag is an ideal receptacle for dropping in feathers and spare parts of the birds you and your hunting buddies are cleaning; dispose of the bag at a roadside collection can or one in the first town you reach.

An alternative is to carry a spade in the trunk and dig a hole for the feather collection. It takes only a minute.

Before starting the actual cleaning, decide whether to skin or pick your birds. It's easier to skin them, but picked birds look better for table service and some game chefs say they taste better. (Frankly, I can't tell the difference; I am always happy if someone else wants to pick birds, but when I have to do the dressing, I skin them.)

Also, decide whether to pull out the breast or to prepare the body for cooking. I'm a breast man because it's faster to dress birds this way, and you lose very little meat by discarding the legs and back. Other hunters are leg men and save everything when preparing a bird.

With a few exceptions, everything in this chapter pertains to whitewings and bandtails as well as to mourning doves. The bandtail weighs about 13 ounces on the wing. Obviously, their drumsticks are larger than those of a 4-ounce dove. The whitewing is about halfway in between. How you prepare your birds is a matter of personal preference, so I will explain how to handle the various options.

A freshly killed dove, whitewing, or pigeon dry picks quickly. (By dry picking we mean removing the feathers without first dunking the bird in water.) At the time you knock a bird down in the field, the feathers come out so easily you can almost rub them off. The longer you wait to dry pick the bird, the more stubborn the feathers are to remove. Young birds pick more easily than old birds. As a general rule of thumb, if you wait more than about three hours to pick a bird, you'll probably have to use hot water or risk tearing the skin off with the feathers.

A 6-gallon bucket is ideal to use for wet picking. Heat the water to a little above 150°, add a tablespoon of detergent, and stir. Grab two or three birds by the feet and dunk; the water should be down to the ideal temperature of 150° by then.

Move the birds up and down in the bucket to force the water through the feathers to the skin. The detergent will cut through the oil on the feathers and allow the hot water to reach the skin and soften it. Usually, you need slosh the birds only about 15 seconds.

Lift the birds and let them drain a couple of seconds. Then rub the feathers off; only the wing and tail feathers will need plucking. Snip the legs off at the knee joint, the wings at the wrist, and the neck about ½ inch from the body.

For cutting off spare parts, the ideal instrument is a pair of stainless steel game shears which you can buy for about $15.00 (the stainless steel prevents rusting). A cheaper substitute is a pair of straight-edged wire cutters you can pick up at a hardware store for about $5.00. The only other instrument you need is a small sharp-pointed knife for cutting, scraping, and prying out lead shot.

For wet picking, some hunters prefer removing the wing tips and lowerlegs before dunking in hot water in order to have that much out of the way first.

After head, wing tips, and lower legs have been removed and the bird rubbed and picked, there are usually a few tufts of feathers left, especially on the rump. I snip the rumps off with shears but some gourmets like to leave them on, as this fatty area contributes extra juices during cooking.

After the bird has been defeathered, place it on its back and remove the crop, located at the intersection of the bottom side of the neck and chest. (Some hunters like to open the crops to see what the birds have been feeding on.)

To remove the insides, make a shallow incision from the tip of the breast or keel bone to and through the rectum. Or simply poke your forefinger through the skin at the tip of the keel bone and gently tear an opening to the rectum.

Up to now, there has been little or no bloodshed, but your time has come! When the body cavity is open, use one to three fingers, whatever you can insert, to run alongside the breast towards the neck. Reach as far as you can and grab the heart and lungs and anything else movable and curve your fingers down until they touch the backbone. Now, pull back towards the body cavity all the way to the rectum. You should come out holding about 98 percent of what needs removing.

Rinse the inside of the bird, and with your fingernails or a knife scrape the length of the backbone to remove lung fragments, blood vessels, and anything stringing loose. Then wash the inside of the bird.

A few hunters save the giblets for cooking, but

they are quite small and need culinary assistance. A friend of mine buys chicken giblets to mix with the doves in cooking. It provokes some surprised comments because a chicken liver or gizzard is nearly as large as a dressed dove.

After all the birds have been washed, use your sharp-pointed knife to dig out embedded shot; reddish purple marks indicate where shot entered. This is a good opportunity to observe the anatomy of birds: notice that the huge breast protects the vital organs from shot penetration and also that most shot does not penetrate inside the body cavity. This will help convince you that most doves killed cleanly are killed by shock, not penetration.

If you're dressing doves indoors, it pays to spread a lot of newspapers. I use a half-section of a sheet, and when it accumulates a supply of feathers, I turn the other half sheet down on top. I have never been able to clean a limit of birds without getting some feather drift. In fact, the tops of our kitchen cabinets probably have several strata of various game bird feathers. One other point—when you set up to process doves, be wary of doors which lead to the outside. I had a kid bust in on me one windy night, and it took two weeks to chase down all the feathers! The last one floated down into my cereal on Easter morning.

For breast pulling, I try to set up an assembly line. First, I snip the wings and necks of all the birds, then I pull the breasts of all of them and finally I pick the shot out. I do as much as I can before getting blood on my hands. Once you do, you can't keep it from welding to feathers, even if you're working in the kitchen sink with the water running.

The wings should be sheared off at the shoulder joint, and are 10 times easier to remove with shears than with a knife. The neck is snipped near the chest. You can perform the breast pulling without removing the neck and head, but I like to get them out of the way.

When all of the birds are snipped, take the first and put it on its back. While holding the bird with one hand, insert the thumb of the other hand into the body cavity at the tip of the keel bone. Work the thumb inside against the breast as far as it will go, and then grasp the outside of the breast with the other fingers. Pull forward firmly to remove the breast. It will come out fairly easily. Everything else remains behind!

At this point, you will be holding a dove breast with the skin and feathers on. Peel the skin off and wash. After you have performed this with all the birds, pick the shot out. That's all there is to it. To skin a whole bird, start by clipping off wings at the shoulder, the neck at the breast, and lower legs at knee joints. Pinch a hole in the skin just about at the tip of the keel bone. Insert a finger and loosen skin in both directions to encircle the bird amidship. Peel the front half of the skin towards the neck and off. Pull off the back skin, working the thighs through. The skin will split at the rump, leaving a tuft of feathers; cut off the rump. Take the insides out and wash.

Finally, put the discarded parts and desecrated newspapers into a large plastic bag and seal the top tightly with a wire; then put this in the regular garbage bag. (In case the garbage collector is late, the plastic bag is a good safety margin.)

If the birds are to be eaten in the next three or four days, they should be handled like any meat: wrap them and store in your refrigerator.

For freezing I generally use a 24-ounce plastic container which will hold 6 or 8 doves, depending on how they are dressed. This helps when I

want to remove only a small number from the freezer. Many hunters cut out part of the top of a gallon milk plastic container, leaving the handle on. This stores a lot of doves, but they all must be thawed at the same time.

Place the doves in a container for freezing, and cover with water about 9/10 of the height of the container, leaving room for ice expansion. Make sure all birds are covered with water so there is no chance of freezer burn.

Before placing in the freezer, be sure to label what is in the container and the number. A felt-tip pen is ideal for labeling and if you have room, you might want to add the date of storage. Proper labeling saves a lot of confusion several months later. I don't go along with a friend of mine who never labels anything. He says he likes to keep the family surprised. He's the same guy who once at an auction bought a wrecked railroad car filled with canned goods with all the labels burned off!

According to experts, game birds, properly frozen, will keep well for a year with no loss in flavor. I suspect they'll keep much longer, but I like to empty my freezer before the start of a new season.

Doves, whitewings, and bandtails all have red meat, which is typical of most migratory birds. Birds that have white meat are usually stay-at-homers like quail, pheasant, and turkey.

Doves and whitewings seldom have a strong, gamey taste, especially those which have been feeding in farm fields. The bandtail, because it feeds mostly on mast crops, has a stronger taste. Some hunters insist on marinating their bandtails overnight in wine or vinegar to tame them down.

There is no way to explain how these three birds taste. It's like trying to tell someone what vanilla ice cream tastes like. What do you compare it to? The only thing to do is try it.

If you have a guest who has never eaten any of the three, he might think the taste is a little sudden. There is no doubt that it's an abrupt change from the bland diet of a poultry market. I have never understood people who want to eat game and then holler that it's too gamey! I have no objection to mellowing the birds a bit with onions, bacon, or wine as long as the basic game taste remains, but why bother at all if you're not willing to honestly try a rich, unique dish?

Most recipes call for doves, whitewings, and bandtails to be cooked until well done. Some experts, or people who know what they like, cook them until the meat falls off the bone, and it's surprising how good they are. I've never run across anyone who cooked them rare as some waterfowlers do their ducks.

A dove breast is pushed hard to weigh two ounces, even soaked in juices. The hostess for a dove dinner may well wonder how many birds to prepare. A good estimation is two mourning doves per guest, with a few spares for seconds. Whitewings are harder to figure; one may be enough for light eaters, but heartier appetites may welcome two. Again, two per guest is a fairly safe estimation. With bandtails, cook one per person with a few spares, assuming you've bagged that many.

A whole pigeon or even a dove breast on a plate is not always easy to handle with a knife and fork. The considerate hostess should laughingly inform guests that it's all right to use their fingers, even if she's experienced enough to get by without doing so. Anyway, most game dinners wind up being informal, whether the hostess planned it that way or not.

Because of the insurance I take out, we've never had guests in for a game dinner which was a failure. The insurance is a bottle of gin and a bottle of vermouth. If the dinner is scheduled for 7:00 p.m., we don't serve the birds until almost 8:00. That gives everyone time to have at least three martinis, and no one has ever complained about our birds. Come to think of it, we could have served fish ducks at some of those meals, and no one would have noticed the difference.

The following recipes will enable you to share the delicious fruits of dove hunting with your family and friends. With some judicious juggling, the meat of white-winged dove or band-tailed pigeons may be substituted for mourning dove meat. (Incidentally, "doves" in the list of ingredients means doves which have been thoroughly cleaned, defeathered, skinned or not, as you prefer, and eviscerated. Reread the first section of Chapter XII if you are in doubt as to how any of these procedures are accomplished.) Many of the recipes may also be expanded or reduced according to the number of guests you plan to serve or the degree of success of your last hunting venture!

We would like to thank the following organizations and individuals for their help in developing, testing, and contributing these culinary offerings: The South Dakota Department of Game, Fish, and Parks; the United States Brewers Association; Mrs. Fred J. Moses of Knoxville, Tennessee; Mrs. J. A. Lauder of Tallahassee, Florida; and especially Miss Lena Sturges, Foods Editor of *Southern Living* magazine.

DOVE HÉLÈNE

8 to 10 doves
1 strip bacon for each dove
1 (3-ounce) package chipped beef
1 (10¾-ounce) can condensed cream of mushroom soup,
1 cup commercial sour cream

Wrap each dove with a strip of bacon. Place a layer of chipped beef in the bottom of a casserole large enough to arrange all the doves in one layer on top of the chipped beef. Pour soup and sour cream over the top of chipped beef and dove. Bake at 350° for 1 hour or until tender. Yield: 6 to 8 servings

FRIED DOVES

Olive oil
Doves
All-purpose flour seasoned with salt and pepper
Onion slices
Water

Put enough olive oil in a heavy skillet to cover the bottom. Coat doves with seasoned flour and brown in oil, adding onion slices. After doves are browned, add a little water to pan and braise on low heat. Cooking time depends on age of birds, but 30 to 45 minutes should be sufficient.

DOVE PIE

12 doves
4 strips bacon (or 2 lean pork chops)
  Salt and pepper
¼ to ½ teaspoon basil
½ teaspoon thyme
  Pastry for double-crust pie, divided
6 tablespoons butter or margarine
4 tablespoons cornstarch
2 tablespoons all-purpose flour
1 pint whipping cream
  Reserved dove cooking liquid
2 tablespoons butter or margarine

Place doves and bacon (or pork chops) in just enough water to cover; bring to a quick boil, reduce heat, and simmer until very tender and liquid is reduced by half. Add salt, pepper, and herbs and simmer 15 minutes longer.

Line a greased 2½ to 3-quart casserole with half the pie crust. Remove doves from cooking liquid, bone, and place pieces in casserole. Prepare sauce by melting butter over low heat, then stirring in cornstarch and flour. When well blended, add whipping cream and reserved dove cooking liquid, and heat until sauce comes to a boil. Pour sauce over dove and place remaining half of the pie crust over all, pressing the 2 crusts together and fluting edges. Slit top for steam to escape and dot 2 tablespoons butter over crust. Bake at 400° for 30 minutes or until golden brown. Yield: 4 to 6 servings.

SMOTHERED DOVES

6 to 8 doves
3 tablespoons all-purpose flour
½ teaspoon salt
¼ teaspoon pepper
½ cup olive oil
1 or 2 garlic cloves
1 cup red wine

Dust doves with flour seasoned with salt and pepper. In a heavy skillet, lightly brown doves in hot oil and garlic. When doves are browned, remove and discard garlic. Add wine and enough water to barely cover birds. Simmer about 1½ hours or until tender. Thicken pan juices with a little remaining seasoned flour. Yield: 3 to 4 servings.

ROASTED DOVES WITH SAUERKRAUT

Doves
Salt
Sauerkraut
Bacon strips

Lightly salt each dove on inside cavity. Stuff with sauerkraut and put bacon strips on top of each bird. Roast at 400° for about 30 minutes or until tender.

DOVE CASSEROLE WITH POLENTA

6 doves
6 small onions
6 teaspoons butter or margarine
Few springs parsley
½ cup butter or margarine
1 clove garlic, crushed
1 (1-pound) can whole tomatoes
1 (6-ounce) can mushrooms
1 large onion, chopped
½ teaspoon thyme
¼ teaspoon dried basil
Parsley
Polenta

Stuff each dove with a small onion, a teaspoon of butter and a few sprigs of parsley. Melt ½ cup butter in skillet and sauté garlic. Remove garlic and reserve. Brown doves quickly in skillet. Place browned doves and remaining ingredients from skillet in a deep casserole and bake at 375° for 1½ hours. Garnish with lemon sections and parsley; serve with polenta. Yield: 4 to 6 servings.

Polenta:

4 cups water
1 cup cornmeal
1 teaspoon salt
2 tablespoons butter or margarine
4 tablespoons grated Parmesan cheese
Dash cayenne pepper
½ teaspoon freshly ground black pepper

Bring water to boil. Slowly add cornmeal and salt and cook, stirring constantly until slightly thickened. Place over boiling water and cook 45 minutes. Add the rest of the ingredients and cook a few minutes more. Spoon polenta around hot platter to make a ring for doves and sauce.

DOVE HASH À LA REITH

About 4 to 6 doves
1 (10½-ounce) can condensed chicken consommé
6 tablespoons butter or margarine, divided
2½ tablespoons all-purpose flour
⅔ cup half-and-half
⅔ cup bread crumbs
⅔ cup chopped green pepper
⅔ cup chopped onion
2 tablespoons chopped parsley
½ teaspoon ground sage
½ teaspoon salt
Freshly ground black pepper to taste
2 ounces sherry

Cook whole doves in chicken consommé until tender. Remove breasts and dice meat. Measure 4 cups and set aside. Melt 3 tablespoons butter or margarine and blend in flour and half-and-half. In another pan, melt remaining butter and sauté bread crumbs, green pepper, onion, parsley, and sage. Mix the sautéed ingredients, flour mixture, and dove meat. Place in skillet. Add salt, pepper, and sherry and cook gently for 25 to 30 minutes. Before serving, place in casserole for a few minutes under the broiler. To keep right consistency while cooking, add pot liquor left from cooking whole doves. Yield: 6 servings.

TEXAS-STYLE DOVES

⅔ cup minced onion
2 cloves garlic, minced
½ bay leaf
1 teaspoon peppercorns
½ cup butter or margarine, melted
6 doves
1 cup white wine
1 cup water
2 cups whipping cream
½ teaspoon salt
⅛ teaspoon pepper
1 teaspoon minced chives

Cook onion, garlic, bay leaf and peppercorns in butter until onion is tender. Add doves and sauté until browned. Add wine and water and simmer for 30 minutes. Remove doves; strain sauce into a 2-quart casserole, and gradually add cream to sauce. Stir remaining seasonings into sauce; add doves. Cover and heat just to boiling. Serve hot. Yield: 3 to 4 servings.

ROAST DOVES

4 doves
  Salt and pepper
4 thin slices lemon, seeded
4 strips bacon, about 2 inches long
¾ cup chicken broth
¾ cup whipping cream
  Parsley jelly (optional)

Rub doves inside and out with salt and pepper, and place a slice of lemon inside each bird. Secure bacon over the breast of each bird. Arrange in a greased casserole, add broth, and bake at 375° for 25 to 30 minutes, basting often. When birds and gravy are a rich brown, pour cream over birds. Return to oven and let cream bubble up in pan about 1 minute, basting twice with sauce. Serve with gravy from the pan and parsley jelly, if desired. Yield: 2 to 4 servings.

DOVE BREASTS STROGANOFF

12 to 18 dove breasts
1 medium onion, chopped
2 tablespoons butter or margarine, melted
1 (10¾-ounce) can condensed cream of celery soup
1 (4-ounce) can mushrooms
½ cup California Sauterne
½ teaspoon oregano
½ teaspoon rosemary
  Salt and pepper to taste
1 teaspoon bottled brown bouquet sauce
1 cup commercial sour cream
  Cooked wild rice

Arrange doves in a large baking dish; do not crowd. Sauté onion in butter. Add remaining ingredients except sour cream and rice. Pour mixture over doves. Cover dish lightly with foil; bake at 325° for 1 hour, turning occasionally. Add sour cream; stir into sauce. Bake, uncovered, an additional 20 minutes. To serve, spoon over wild rice. Yield: 6 to 9 servings.

WHITE-WINGED DOVE ITALIENNE

4 doves
  All-purpose flour seasoned with garlic
  Salt and pepper
¼ cup olive oil
1 (8-ounce) can tomato sauce
½ cup beer
4 medium onions, sliced
¼ teaspoon oregano
3 tablespoons chopped parsley

Sprinkle doves inside and out with seasoned flour and salt and pepper. Heat olive oil in heavy skillet; add doves and brown on all sides. Add tomato sauce, beer, onions, and oregano. Bring to a boil. Cover and cook over low heat 30 to 45 minutes or until tender. Just before serving, stir in parsley. Yield: 2 to 4 servings.

DOVES BRAZOS VALLEY

- 6 doves
- ¾ cup butter or margarine, melted
- 1 tablespoon Worcestershire sauce
- 1 teaspoon garlic salt
- ⅓ cup cooking sherry
- 1 cup (canned or fresh) chopped mushrooms
- ½ teaspoon ground nutmeg
- Salt and pepper to taste
- ⅓ cup all-purpose flour
- Toast
- Fresh grapes

Brown doves on all sides in melted butter in a large skillet. Add remaining ingredients except flour, toast, and grapes and cover skillet. Allow to simmer for about 20 minutes; remove the doves from the skillet; add flour to the sauce, cooking and stirring until it is browned. Place doves on toast and top with sauce. Garnish with fresh grapes. Yield: 3 servings.

JODIE'S COMPANY DOVES

- 12 doves
- All-purpose flour seasoned with salt and pepper
- Garlic salt
- 1 cup butter or margarine
- Bottled brown bouquet sauce
- 1 (1⅜-ounce) package dry onion soup mix
- Steamed rice

Roll doves in seasoned flour; sprinkle each dove with garlic salt. Melt 1 cup butter in heavy iron skillet, add doves at medium heat, and keep turning until brown. Add enough warm water to almost cover the doves, and then add 2 or 3 teaspoons bottled brown bouquet sauce to make instant rich gravy and stir. Sprinkle dry onion soup mix evenly over the doves. Cover and simmer about 2 hours. Serve with steamed rice. Yield: 6 to 8 servings.

Appendix

The following 32 states had open hunting seasons for mourning dove during the 1975–76 season. The five states marked "1." had white-winged dove seasons; those marked "2." had band-tailed pigeon seasons. The final season dates and bag limits are usually announced in August although some states have traditional opening days each year.

For information on state-managed areas, licenses, and regulations contact the game and fish agency of the state you plan to hunt in. The states have cooperative agreements with various federal agencies which open their lands to public hunting.

Some of the states have their own regulations in addition to federal regulations and the hunter is responsible for obeying all of them. It pays to check before you go. The regulations are subject to change each year.

A federal migratory bird hunting stamp is not required for doves and pigeons, but some states require a special band-tailed pigeon permit. Others require a special permit for hunting state wildlife management areas.

STATE GAME AND FISH AGENCIES

Alabama: Division of Game and Fish, Department of Conservation and Natural Resources, 64 North Union Street, Montgomery 36104

1., 2. Arizona: Game and Fish Department, 2222 West Greenway, Phoenix 85023

Arkansas: Game and Fish Commission, Game and Fish Commission Building, Little Rock 72201

1., 2. California: Department of Fish and Game, The Resources Agency, 1416 Ninth Street, Sacramento 95814

2. Colorado: Division of Wildlife, 6060 Broadway, Denver 80216

Delaware: Division of Fish and Wildlife, Department of Natural Resources and Environmental Control, The Edward Tatnall Building, Legislative Avenue and William Penn Street, Dover 19901

Florida: Game and Fresh Water Fish Commission, 620 South Meridian Street, Tallahassee 32304

Georgia: Game and Fish Division, Department of Natural Resources, 270 Washington Street S.W., Atlanta 30334

Hawaii: Division of Fish and Game, 1179 Punchbowl Street, Honolulu 96813

Idaho: Fish and Game Department, 600 South Walnut Street, Box 25, Boise 83707

Illinois: Division of Wildlife Resources, Department of Conservation, 602 State Office Building, Springfield 62706

Kansas: Forestry, Fish, and Game Commission, Box 1028, Pratt 67124

Kentucky: Department of Fish and Wildlife Resources, Capitol Plaza Tower, Frankfort 40601

Louisiana: Wildlife and Fisheries Commission, 400 Royal Street, New Orleans 70130

Maryland: Wildlife Administration, Department of Natural Resources, Tawes State Office Building, Annapolis 21401

Mississippi: Game and Fish Commission, Robert E. Lee Office Building, 239 North Lamar Street, Box 451, Jackson 39205

Missouri: Wildlife Division, Department of Conservation, P.O. Box 180, Jefferson City 65101

1. Nevada: Department of Fish and Game, Box 10678, Reno 89510

1., 2. New Mexico: Department of Game and Fish, State Capitol, Sante Fe 87503

North Carolina: Division of Game, Wildlife Resources Commission, Albemarle Building, 325 North Salisbury Street, Raleigh 27611

Oklahoma: Game Division, Department of Wildlife Conservation, 1801 North Lincoln, P.O. Box 53465, Oklahoma City 73105

2. Oregon: State Wildlife Commission, Box 3503, Portland 97208

Pennsylvania: Game Commission, P.O. Box 1567, Harrisburg 17120

Rhode Island: Division of Fish and Wildlife, Department of Natural Resources, 83 Park Street, Providence 02903

South Carolina: Wildlife and Marine Resources Department, Building D, Dutch Plaza, Box 167, Columbia 29202

Tennessee: Tennessee Wildlife Resources Agency, P.O. Box 40747, Ellington Agricultural Center, Nashville 37204

1. Texas: Parks and Wildlife Department, John H. Reagan Building, Austin 78701

2. Utah: Division of Wildlife Resources, 1596 West North Temple Street, Salt Lake City 84116

Virginia: Commission of Game and Inland Fisheries, 4010 West Broad Street, Box 11104, Richmond 23230

2. Washington: Department of Game, 600 N. Capitol Way, Olympia 98504

West Virginia: Game Management, Department of Natural Resources, 1800 Washington Street, East, Charleston 25305

Wyoming: Game and Fish Department, 5400 Bishop Boulevard, Cheyenne 82001

The Fish and Wildlife Service, U.S. Department of the Interior, is charged with protection of migratory game birds. The Secretary of Interior annually sets hunting regulations in cooperation with state agencies.

For administrative purposes, the Fish and Wildlife Service has headquarters in Washington and has six regional offices plus Alaska. For a free copy of the federal hunting regulations for doves and wild pigeons, you may write the director in Washington but you may get a quicker reply by contacting the office for your region as listed below. The federal regulations list the seasons, shooting hours, and bag limits for all the states and this is most helpful if you plan to hunt in states other than your home state.

If you do, when you write for the current hunting regulations, you should also ask for free copies of *other* federal laws and regulations governing the interstate shipment and transportation of game and fish. You can take or ship a legal possession of birds back to your home, but you must obey the regulations or be subject to strict penalties.

To encourage you to know and follow all regulations, Charley would like to remind you that violations of selling and bartering provisions of The Migratory Bird Treaty Act can lead to a fine of not more than $2,000, imprisonment for not more than two years, or both. The Feds will inconvenience you!

When you contact the regional offices of United States Fish and Wildlife Service, you may wish to ask about wildlife refuges and other federal lands which are open to the public for dove hunting. The address is as follows: United States Fish and Wildlife Service Director, United States Fish and Wildlife Service, Department of the Interior, Washington, D.C. 20240

REGIONAL OFFICES

Region 1 (California, Hawaii, Idaho, Nevada, Oregon, and Washington): 1500 N.E. Irving Street (P.O. Box 3737), Portland, Oregon 97208

Region 2 (Arizona, New Mexico, Oklahoma, and Texas): 500 Gold Avenue S.W. (P.O. Box 1306), Albuquerque, New Mexico 87103

Region 3 (Illinois, Indiana, Michigan, Minnesota, Ohio, and Wisconsin): Federal Building, Fort Snelling, Twin Cities, Minnesota 55111

Region 4 (Alabama, Arkansas, Florida, Georgia, Kentucky, Louisiana, Mississippi, North Carolina, South Carolina, Puerto Rico, Tennessee, and the Virgin Islands): 17 Executive Park Drive N.E., Atlanta, Georgia 30329

Region 5 (Connecticut, Delaware, Maine, Maryland, Massachusetts, New Hampshire, New Jersey, New York, Pennsylvania, Rhode Island, Vermont, Virginia, and West Virginia): U.S. Post Office and Courthouse, Boston, Massachusetts 02109

Region 6 (Colorado, Iowa, Kansas, Missouri, Montana, Nebraska, North Dakota, South Dakota, Utah, and Wyoming): P.O. Box 25486 Denver Federal Center, Denver, Colorado 80225

BUREAU OF LAND MANAGEMENT

Director, Bureau of Land Management, Department of the Interior, Washington, D.C. 20240. National Headquarters.

STATE OFFICES IN DOVE STATES

Arizona: BLM, Federal Building, Rm. 3022, Phoenix 85025

California: BLM, Federal Office Building, Rm. E-2841, 2800 Cottage Way, Sacramento 95825

Colorado: BLM, Rm. 700, Colorado State Bank Building, 1600 Broadway, Denver 80202

Idaho: BLM, 398 Federal Building, 550 West Fort Street, Boise 83724

Nevada: BLM, Federal Building, Rm. 3008, 300 Booth Street, Reno 89502

New Mexico: BLM, Federal Building, South Federal Place, Santa Fe 87501

Oregon and Washington: BLM, 729 N.E. Oregon Street, P.O. Box 2965, Portland, 97208

Utah: BLM, Federal Building, 125 South State, P.O. Box 11505, Salt Lake City 84111

Wyoming: BLM, Joseph C. O'Mahoney Federal Center, Cheyenne 82001